The Love Affairs of a Bibliomaniac

by Eugene Field

Originally published in 1895.

INTRODUCTION

The determination to found a story or a series of sketches on the delights, adventures and misadventures connected with bibliomania did not come impulsively to my brother. For many years, in short during the greater part of nearly a quarter of a century of journalistic work, he had celebrated in prose and verse, and always in his happiest and most delightful vein, the pleasures of book-hunting. Himself an indefatigable collector of books, the possessor of a library as valuable as it was interesting, a library containing volumes obtained only at the cost of great personal sacrifice, he was in the most active sympathy with the disease called bibliomania, and knew, as few comparatively poor men have known, the half-pathetic, half-humorous side of that incurable mental infirmity.

The newspaper column, to which he contributed almost daily for twelve years, comprehended many sly digs and gentle scoffings at those of his unhappy fellow citizens who became notorious, through his instrumentality, in their devotion to old book-shelves and auction sales. And all the time none was more assiduous than this same good-natured cynic in running down a mighty prize, no matter what its cost or what the attending difficulties. "I save others, myself I cannot save," was his humorous cry.

In his published writings are many evidences of my brother's appreciation of what he has somewhere characterized the "soothing affliction of bibliomania." Nothing of book-hunting lore has been more happily expressed than "The Bibliomaniac's Prayer," in which the troubled petitioner fervently asserts:

"But if, O Lord, it pleaseth Thee

To keep me in temptation's way,

I humbly ask that I may be

Most notably beset to-day;

Let my temptation be a book,

Which I shall purchase, hold and keep,

Whereon, when other men shall look,

They'll wail to know I got it cheap."

And again, in "The Bibliomaniac's Bride," nothing breathes better the spirit of the incurable patient than this:

"Prose for me when I wished for prose,

Verse when to verse inclined,—

Forever bringing sweet repose

To body, heart and mind.

Oh, I should bind this priceless prize

In bindings full and fine,

And keep her where no human eyes

Should see her charms, but ...ine!"

In "Dear Old London" the ... et wailed that "a splendid Horace cheap for cash" lau... ...ed at his poverty, and in "Dibdin's Ghost" he revell... in the delights that await the bibliomaniac in the future ... ...te, where there is no admission to the women fo... who, "wanting victuals, make a fuss if we buy books inst... ...d"; while in "Flail, Trask and Bisland" is the very essenc... ...of bibliomania, the unquenchable thirst for pos... ...ssion. And yet, despite these self-accusations, bibliophil... rather than bibliomania would be the word to characterize ...is conscientious purpose. If he purchased quaint and rare b... ...oks it was to own them to the full extent, inwardly as we... ...s outwardly. The mania for books kept him continually ...uying; the love of books supervened to make them a... ...art of himself and his life.

Toward the close of Augus... ...of the present year my brother wrote the first chapter of "... ...e Love Affairs of a Bibliomaniac." At that tim... ...e was in an exhausted physical condition and app... ...ently unfit for any protracted literary labor. But the pros... ...ct of gratifying a long-cherished ambition, the de... ...ht of beginning the story he had planned so hopefully, ...med to give him new strength, and he threw him... ...lf into the work with an enthusiasm that was, alas, ... sleading to those who had noted fearfully his declinin... vigor of body. For years no literary occupation had see... ...ed to give him equal pleasure, and in the discussion of the ... rogress of his writing from day to day his eye would b... ...hten, all of his old animation would return, and everythin... would betray the lively interest he felt in the creatu... of his imagination in whom he was living over the deli... ...ts of the book-hunter's chase. It was his ardent wish that ... ...s work, for the fulfilment of which he had been so long preparing, should be, as he playfully expressed it, a monument of apologetic compensation to a class of people he had so humorously maligned, and those who knew him intimately will recognize in the shortcomings of the bibliomaniac the humble confession of his own weaknesses.

It is easy to understand from the very nature of the undertaking that it was practically limitless; that a bibliomaniac of so many years' experience could prattle on indefinitely concerning his "love affairs," and at the same time be in no danger of repetition. Indeed my brother's plans at the outset were not definitely formed. He would say, when questioned or joked about these amours, that he was in the easy position of Sam Weller when he indited his famous valentine, and could "pull up" at any moment. One week he would contend that a book-hunter ought to be good for a year at least, and the next week he would argue as strongly that it was time to send the old man into winter quarters and go to press. But though the approach of cold weather increased his physical indisposition, he was not the less interested in his prescribed hours of labor, howbeit his weakness warned him that he should say to his book, as his much-loved Horace had written:

"Fuge quo descendere gestis:

Non erit emisso reditis tibi."

Was it strange that his heart should relent, and that he should write on, unwilling to give the word of dismissal to the book whose preparation had been a work of such love and solace?

During the afternoon of Sa[...]day, November 2, the nineteenth instalment of "T[...] Love Affairs" was written. It was the conclusion of his l[...]rary life. The verses supposably contributed by [...]dge Methuen's friend, with which the chapter ends, we[...] the last words written by Eugene Field. He was at th[...] time apparently quite as well as on any day during the fa[...] months, and neither he nor any member of his family [...] the slightest premonition that death was hovering about t[...] household. The next day, though still feeling indispo[...]d, he was at times up and about, always cheerful and [...]ll of that sweetness and sunshine which, in his last [...]ars, seem now to have been the preparation for the life [...]yond. He spoke of the chapter he had written the day befo[...], and it was then that he outlined his plan of comple[...]ng the work. One chapter only remained to be written, and[...] was to chronicle the death of the old bibliomaniac, but n[...] until he had unexpectedly fallen heir to a very rare an[...] almost priceless copy of Horace, which acquisition [...]rked the pinnacle of the book-hunter's conquest. True to [...] love for the Sabine singer, the western poet characteri[...]d the immortal odes of twenty centuries gone the greatest [...]ppiness of bibliomania.

In the early morning of No[...]mber 4 the soul of Eugene Field passed upward. On th[...] table, folded and sealed, were the memoirs of the old mar[...] pon whom the sentence of death had been pronounced[...] On the bed in the corner of the room, with one arm thrown[...] ver his breast, and the smile of peace and rest on his tranq[...] face, the poet lay. All around him, on the shelves and in [...] cases, were the books he loved so well. Ah, who sha[...] say that on that morning his fancy was not verified, and [...] at as the gray light came reverently through the wind[...]w, those cherished volumes did not bestir themselves, a[...] aiting the cheery voice: "Good day to you, my sweet frien[...]. How lovingly they beam upon me, and how glad they are that my rest has been unbroken."

Could they beam upon you less lovingly, great heart, in the chamber warmed by your affection and now sanctified by death? Were they less glad to know that the repose would be unbroken forevermore, since it came the glorious reward, my brother, of the friend who went gladly to it through his faith, having striven for it through his works?

ROSWELL MARTIN FIELD

Buena Park, December, 1895.

The Chapters in this Book

I MY FIRST LOVE

II THE BIRTH OF A NEW PASSION

III THE LUXURY OF READING IN BED

IV THE MANIA OF COLLECTING SEIZES ME

V BALDNESS AND INTELLECTUALITY

VI MY ROMANCE WITH FIAMMETTA

VII THE DELIGHTS OF FENDER-FISHING

VIII BALLADS AND THEIR MAKERS

IX BOOKSELLERS AND PRINTERS, OLD AND NEW

X WHEN FANCHONETTE BEWITCHED ME

XI DIAGNOSIS OF THE BACILLUS LIBRORUM

XII THE PLEASURES OF EXTRA-ILLUSTRATION

XIII ON THE ODORS WHICH MY BOOKS EXHALE

XIV ELZEVIRS AND DIVERS OTHER MATTERS

XV A BOOK THAT BRINGS SOLACE AND CHEER

XVI THE MALADY CALLED CATALOGITIS

XVII THE NAPOLEONIC RENAISSANCE

XVIII MY WORKSHOP AND OTHERS

XIX OUR DEBT TO MONKISH MEN

I

MY FIRST LOVE

At this moment, when I am about to begin the most important undertaking of my life, I recall the sense of abhorrence with which I have at different times read the confessions of men famed for their prowess in the realm of love. These boastings have always shocked me, for I reverence love as the noblest of the passions, and it is impossible for me to conceive how one who has truly fallen victim to its benign influence can ever thereafter speak flippantly of it.

Yet there have been, and there still are, many who take a seeming delight in telling how many conquests they have made, and they not infrequently have the bad taste to explain with wearisome prolixity the ways and the means whereby those conquests were wrought; as, forsooth, an unfeeling huntsman is forever boasting of the game he has slaughtered and is forever expatiating upon the repulsive details of his butcheries.

I have always contended that one who is in love (and having once been in love is to be always in love) has, actually, no confession to make. Love is so guileless, so proper, so pure a passion as to involve none of those things which require or which admit of confession. He, therefore, who surmises that in this exposition of my affaires du coeur there is to be any betrayal of confidences, or any discussion, suggestion, or hint likely either to shame love or its votaries or to bring a blush to the cheek of the fastidious—he is grievously in error.

Nor am I going to boast; for I have made no conquests. I am in no sense a hero. For many, very many years I have walked in a pleasant garden, enjoying sweet odors and soothing spectacles; no predetermined itinerary has controlled my course; I have wandered whither I pleased, and very many times I have strayed so far into the tanglewood and thickets as almost to have lost my way. And now it is my purpose to walk that pleasant garden once more, inviting you to bear me company and to share with me what satisfaction may accrue from an old man's return to old-time places and old-time loves.

As a child I was serious-minded. I cared little for those sports which usually excite the ardor of youth. To out-of-door games and exercises I had particular aversion. I was born in a southern latitude, but at the age of six years I went to live with my grandmother in New Hampshire, both my parents having fallen victims to the cholera. This change from the balmy temperature of the South to the rigors of the North was not agreeable to me, and I have always held it responsible for that delicate health which has attended me through life.

My grandmother encouraged my disinclination to play; she recognized in me that certain seriousness of mind which I remember to have heard her say I inherited from her, and she determined to make of me what she had failed to make of any of her own sons—a professional expounder of the only true faith of Congregationalism. For this reason, and for the further reason that at the tender age of seven years I publicly avowed my desire to become a clergyman, an ambition wholly sincere at that time—for these reasons was I duly installed as prime favorite in my grandmother's affections.

As distinctly as though it were but yesterday do I recall the time when I met my first love. It was in the front room of the old homestead, and the day was a day in spring. The front room answered those purposes which are served by the so-called parlor of the present time. I remember the low ceiling, the big fireplace, the long, broad mantelpiece, the andirons and fender of brass, the tall clock with its jocund and roseate moon, the bellows that was always wheezy, the wax flowers under a glass globe in the corner, an allegorical picture of Solomon's temple, another picture of little Samuel at prayer, the high, stiff-back chairs, the footstool with its gayly embroidered top, the mirror in its gilt-and-black frame—all these things I remember well, and with feelings of tender reverence, and yet that day I now recall was well-nigh threescore and ten years ago!

Best of all I remember the case in which my grandmother kept her books, a mahogany structure, massive and dark, with doors composed of diamond-shaped figures of glass cunningly set in a framework of lead. I was in my seventh year then, and I had learned to read I know not when. The back and current numbers of the "Well-Spring" had fallen prey to my insatiable appetite for literature. With the story of the small boy who stole pin, repented of and confessed that crime, and then became a good and great man, I was as familiar as if I myself had invented that ingenious and instructive tale; I could lisp the moral numbers of Watts, and the didactic hymns of Wesley, and the annual reports of the American Tract Society had already revealed to me the sphere of usefulness in which my grandmother hoped I would ultimately figure with discretion and zeal. And yet my heart was free; wholly untouched of that gentle yet deathless passion which was to become my delight, my inspiration, and my solace, awaited the coming of its first love.

Upon one of those shelves yonder—it is the third shelf from the top, fourth compartment to the right—is that old copy of the "New England Primer," a curious little, thin, square book in faded blue board covers. A good many times I have wondered whether I ought not to have the precious little thing sumptuously attired in the finest style known to my binder; indeed, I have often been tempted to exchange the homely blue board covers for flexible levant, for it occurred to me that in this way I could testify to my regard for the treasured volume. I spoke of this one day to my friend Judge Methuen, for I have great respect for his judgment.

"It would be a desecration," said he, "to deprive the book of its original binding. What! Would you tear off and cast away the covers which have felt the caressing pressure of the hands of those whose memory you revere? The most sacred of sentiments should forbid that act of vandalism!"

I never think or speak of the "New England Primer" that I do not recall Captivity Waite, for it was Captivity who introduced me to the Primer that day in the springtime of sixty-three years ago. She was of my age, a bright, pretty girl—a very pretty, an exceptionally pretty girl, as girls go. We belonged to the same Sunday-school class. I remember that upon this particular day she brought me a russet apple. It was she who discovered the Primer in the mahogany case, and what was not our joy as we turned over the tiny pages together and feasted our eyes upon the vivid pictures and perused the absorbingly interesting text! What wonder that together we wept tears of sympathy at the harrowing recital of the fate of John Rogers!

Even at this remote date I cannot recall that experience with Captivity, involving as it did the wood-cut

representing the unfortunat[...] Rogers standing in an
impossible bonfire and bei[ng ...] consumed thereby in the
presence of his wife and th[e ...] numerous progeny, strung
along in a pitiful line acros[s ...t]he picture for artistic effect—
even now, I say, I cannot c[on]template that experience and
that wood-cut without feeli[ng] lumpy in my throat and moist
about my eyes.

How lasting are the impres[sio]ns made upon the youthful
mind! Through the many b[us]y years that have elapsed since
first I tasted the thrilling sw[ee]ts of that miniature Primer I
have not forgotten that "yo[un]g Obadias, David, Josias, all
were pious"; that "Zaccheu[s h]e did climb the Tree our Lord
to see"; and that "Vashti fo[r] 'ride was set aside"; and still
with many a sympathetic s[hu]dder and tingle do I recall
Captivity's overpowering s[en]se of horror, and mine, as we
lingered long over the port[rai]tures of Timothy flying from
Sin, of Xerxes laid out in f[un]eral garb, and of proud
Korah's troop partly subme[rg]ed.

My Book and Heart

Must never part.

So runs one of the couplets [in] this little Primer-book, and
right truly can I say that fro[m] the springtime day sixty-odd
years ago, when first my he[ar]t went out in love to this little
book, no change of scene o[r] of custom no allurement of
fashion, no demand of mat[ure] years, has abated that love.
And herein is exemplified t[he] advantage which the love of
books has over the other ki[nd]s of love. Women are by
nature fickle, and so are m[en]; their friendships are liable to

dissipation at the merest provocation or the slightest pretext.

Not so, however, with books, for books cannot change. A thousand years hence they are what you find them to-day, speaking the same words, holding forth the same cheer, the same promise, the same comfort; always constant, laughing with those who laugh and weeping with those who weep.

Captivity Waite was an exception to the rule governing her sex. In all candor I must say that she approached closely to a realization of the ideals of a book—a sixteenmo, if you please, fair to look upon, of clear, clean type, well ordered and well edited, amply margined, neatly bound; a human book whose text, as represented by her disposition and her mind, corresponded felicitously with the comeliness of her exterior. This child was the great-great-granddaughter of Benjamin Waite, whose family was carried off by Indians in 1677. Benjamin followed the party to Canada, and after many months of search found and ransomed the captives.

The historian has properly said that the names of Benjamin Waite and his companion in their perilous journey through the wilderness to Canada should "be memorable in all the sad or happy homes of this Connecticut valley forever." The child who was my friend in youth, and to whom I may allude occasionally hereafter in my narrative, bore the name of one of the survivors of this Indian outrage, a name to be revered as a remembrancer of sacrifice and heroism.

II

THE BIRTH O[F] A NEW PASSION

When I was thirteen years [ol]d I went to visit my Uncle Cephas. My grandmother [wo]uld not have parted with me even for that fortnight had [sh]e not actually been compelled to. It happened that she wa[s c]alled to a meeting of the American Tract Society, ar[nd] it was her intention to pay a visit to her cousin, Royall [We]stman, after she had discharged the first and im[pe]rative duty she owed the society. Mrs. Deacon Rann[ey] was to have taken me and provided for my temporal a[nd] spiritual wants during grandmother's absence, bu[t a]t the last moment the deacon came down with one of his [sp]ells of quinsy, and no other alternative remained but to [pa]ck me off to Nashua, where my Uncle Cephas lived.

This involved considerable [e]xpense, for the stage fare was three shillings each way: it [ca]me particularly hard on grandmother, inasmuch as [sh]e had just paid her road tax and had not yet received he[r s]emi-annual dividends on her Fitchburg Railway stock. I[nd]ifferent, however, to every sense of extravagance and [to] all other considerations except those of personal pride, I r[od]e away atop of the stage-coach, full of exultation. A[s w]e rattled past the Waite house I waved my cap to Captivit[y a]nd indulged in the pleasing hope that she would be lon[es]ome without me. Much of the satisfaction of going away [ari]ses from the thought that those you leave behind are [lik]ely to be wretchedly miserable during your abse[nc]e.

My Uncle Cephas lived in a house so very different from my grandmother's that it took me some time to get used to the place. Uncle Cephas was a lawyer, and his style of living was not at all like grandmother's; he was to have been a minister, but at twelve years of age he attended the county fair, and that incident seemed to change the whole bent of his life. At twenty-one he married Samantha Talbott, and that was another blow to grandmother, who always declared that the Talbotts were a shiftless lot. However, I was agreeably impressed with Uncle Cephas and Aunt 'Manthy, for they welcomed me very cordially and turned me over to my little cousins, Mary and Henry, and bade us three make merry to the best of our ability. These first favorable impressions of my uncle's family were confirmed when I discovered that for supper we had hot biscuit and dried beef warmed up in cream gravy, a diet which, with all due respect to grandmother, I considered much more desirable than dry bread and dried-apple sauce.

Aha, old Crusoe! I see thee now in yonder case smiling out upon me as cheerily as thou didst smile those many years ago when to a little boy thou broughtest the message of Romance! And I do love thee still, and I shall always love thee, not only for thy benefaction in those ancient days, but also for the light and the cheer which thy genius brings to all ages and conditions of humanity.

My Uncle Cephas's library was stored with a large variety of pleasing literature. I did not observe a glut of theological publications, and I will admit that I felt somewhat aggrieved personally when, in answer to my inquiry, I was told that there was no "New England Primer" in the collection. But this feeling was soon dissipated by the absorbing interest I took in De Foe's masterpiece, a work unparalleled in the realm of fiction.

I shall not say that "Robins [...] Crusoe" supplanted the
Primer in my affections; th [...] would not be true. I prefer to
say what is the truth; it was [...] my second love. Here again we
behold another advantage v [...] ich the lover of books has
over the lover of women. I [...] e be a genuine lover he can
and should love any numbe [...] of books, and this
polybibliophily is not to the [...] disparagement of any one of
that number. But it is held [...] the expounders of our civil
and our moral laws that he [...] who loveth one woman to the
exclusion of all other wom [...] speaketh by that action the
best and highest praise botl [...] of his own sex and of hers.

I thank God continually tha [...] it hath been my lot in life to
found an empire in my hea [...] —no cramped and wizened
borough wherein one jealo [...] mistress hath exercised her
petty tyranny, but an expan [...] ve and ever-widening
continent divided and subd [...] ided into dominions,
jurisdictions, caliphates, ch [...] fdoms, seneschalships, and
prefectures, wherein tetrarc [...] , burgraves, maharajahs,
palatines, seigniors, caziqu [...] , nabobs, emirs, nizams, and
nawabs hold sway, each ov [...] his special and particular
realm, and all bound togetl [...] in harmonious cooperation by
the conciliating spirit of po [...] bibliophily!

Let me not be misunderstoc [...] ; for I am not a woman-hater. I
do not regret the acquainta [...] es—nay, the friendships—I
have formed with individu: [...] of the other sex. As a
philosopher it has behoove [...] ne to study womankind, else I
should not have appreciate [...] he worth of these other better
loves. Moreover, I take ple [...] ure in my age in associating
this precious volume or tha [...] with one woman or another
whose friendship came inte [...] ny life at the time when I was
reading and loved that boo [...]

The other day I found my nephew William swinging in the hammock on the porch with his girl friend Celia; I saw that the young people were reading Ovid. "My children," said I, "count this day a happy one. In the years of after life neither of you will speak or think of Ovid and his tender verses without recalling at the same moment how of a gracious afternoon in distant time you sat side by side contemplating the ineffably precious promises of maturity and love."

I am not sure that I do not approve that article in Judge Methuen's creed which insists that in this life of ours woman serves a probationary period for sins of omission or of commission in a previous existence, and that woman's next step upward toward the final eternity of bliss is a period of longer or of shorter duration, in which her soul enters into a book to be petted, fondled, beloved and cherished by some good man—like the Judge, or like myself, for that matter.

This theory is not an unpleasant one; I regard it as much more acceptable than those so-called scientific demonstrations which would make us suppose that we are descended from tree-climbing and bug-eating simians. However, it is far from my purpose to enter upon any argument of these questions at this time, for Judge Methuen himself is going to write a book upon the subject, and the edition is to be limited to two numbered and signed copies upon Japanese vellum, of which I am to have one and the Judge the other.

The impression I made upon Uncle Cephas must have been favorable, for when my next birthday rolled around there came with it a book from Uncle Cephas—my third love, Grimm's "Household Stories." With the perusal of this monumental work was born that passion for fairy tales and folklore which increased rather than diminished with my maturer years. Even at the present time I delight in a good fairy story, and I am grateful to Lang and to Jacobs for the benefit they have conferred upon me and the rest of English-reading humanity through the medium of the fairy books and the folk tales they have translated and compiled. Baring-Gould and Lady Wilde have done noble work in the same realm; the writings of the former have interested me particularly, for together with profound learning in directions which are specially pleasing to me, Baring-Gould has a distinct literary touch which invests his work with a grace indefinable but delicious and persuasive.

I am so great a lover of and believer in fairy tales that I once organized a society for the dissemination of fairy literature, and at the first meeting of this society we resolved to demand of the board of education to drop mathematics from the curriculum in the public schools and to substitute therefor a four years' course in fairy literature, to be followed, if the pupil desired, by a post-graduate course in demonology and folk-lore. We hired and fitted up large rooms, and the cause seemed to be flourishing until the second month's rent fell due. It was then discovered that the treasury was empty; and with this discovery the society ended its existence, without having accomplished any tangible result other than the purchase of a number of sofas and chairs, for which Judge Methuen and I had to pay.

Still, I am of the opinion (and Judge Methuen indorses it) that we need in this country of ours just that influence which the fairy tale exerts. We are becoming too practical; the lust for material gain is throttling every other consideration. Our babes and sucklings are no longer regaled with the soothing tales of giants, ogres, witches, and fairies; their hungry, receptive minds are filled with stories about the pursuit and slaughter of unoffending animals, of war and of murder, and of those questionable practices whereby a hero is enriched and others are impoverished. Before he is out of his swaddling-cloth the modern youngster is convinced that the one noble purpose in life is to get, get, get, and keep on getting of worldly material. The fairy tale is tabooed because, as the sordid parent alleges, it makes youth unpractical.

One consequence of this deplorable condition is, as I have noticed (and as Judge Methuen has, too), that the human eye is diminishing in size and fulness, and is losing its lustre. By as much as you take the God-given grace of fancy from man, by so much do you impoverish his eyes. The eye is so beautiful and serves so very many noble purposes, and is, too, so ready in the expression of tenderness, of pity, of love, of solicitude, of compassion, of dignity, of every gentle mood and noble inspiration, that in that metaphor which contemplates the eternal vigilance of the Almighty we recognize the best poetic expression of the highest human wisdom.

My nephew Timothy has three children, two boys and a girl. The elder boy and the girl have small black eyes; they are as devoid of fancy as a napkin is of red corpuscles; they put their pennies into a tin bank, and they have won all the marbles and jack-stones in the neighborhood. They do not believe in Santa Claus or in fairies or in witches; they know that two nickels make a dime, and their golden rule is to do others as others would do them. The other boy (he has been christened Matthew, after me) has a pair of large, round, deep-blue eyes, expressive of all those emotions which a keen, active fancy begets.

Matthew can never get his l of fairy tales, and how the
dear little fellow loves San Claus! He sees things at night;
he will not go to bed in the ark; he hears and understands
what the birds and crickets y, and what the night wind
sings, and what the rustling aves tell. Wherever Matthew
goes he sees beautiful pictu s and hears sweet music; to
his impressionable soul all ture speaks its wisdom and its
poetry. God! how I love the boy! And he shall never
starve! A goodly share of v at I have shall go to him! But
this clause in my will, which the Judge recently drew for
me, will, I warrant me, give he dear child the greatest
happiness:

"Item. To my beloved gran ephew and namesake,
Matthew, I do bequeath an give (in addition to the lands
devised and the stocks, bon and moneys willed to him, as
hereinabove specified) the o mahogany bookcases
numbered 11 and 13, and tl contents thereof, being
volumes of fairy and folk t s of all nations, and
dictionaries and other treat s upon demonology,
witchcraft, mythology, mag and kindred subjects, to be
his, his heirs, and his assign forever."

III

THE LUXURY OF READING IN BED

Last night, having written what you have just read about the benefits of fairy literature, I bethought me to renew my acquaintance with some of those tales which so often have delighted and solaced me. So I piled at least twenty chosen volumes on the table at the head of my bed, and I daresay it was nigh daylight when I fell asleep. I began my entertainment with several pages from Keightley's "Fairy Mythology," and followed it up with random bits from Crofton Croker's "Traditions of the South of Ireland," Mrs. Carey's "Legends of the French Provinces," Andrew Lang's Green, Blue and Red fairy books, Laboulaye's "Last Fairy Tales," Hauff's "The Inn in the Spessart," Julia Goddard's "Golden Weathercock," Frere's "Eastern Fairy Legends," Asbjornsen's "Folk Tales," Susan Pindar's "Midsummer Fays," Nisbit Bain's "Cossack Fairy Tales," etc., etc.

I fell asleep with a copy of Villamaria's fairy stories in my hands, and I had a delightful dream wherein, under the protection and guidance of my fairy godmother, I undertook the rescue of a beautiful princess who had been enchanted by a cruel witch and was kept in prison by the witch's son, a hideous ogre with seven heads, whose companions were four equally hideous dragons.

This undertaking in which I was engaged involved a period of five years, but time is of precious little consideration to one when he is dreaming of exploits achieved in behalf of a beautiful princess. My fairy godmother (she wore a mob-cap and was hunchbacked) took good care of me, and

conducted me safely throu[...] all my encounters with
demons, giants, dragons, w[...]hes, serpents, hippogriffins,
ogres, etc.; and I had just r[...]ued the princess and broken
the spell which bound her, [...]d we were about to "live in
peace to the end of our live[...]" when I awoke to find it was
all a dream, and that the ga[...]ight over my bed had been
blazing away during the en[...]e period of my five-year war
for the delectable maiden.

This incident gives me an [...]ortunity to say that
observation has convinced [...]e that all good and true book-
lovers practise the pleasing [...]nd improving avocation of
reading in bed. Indeed, I fu[...] believe with Judge Methuen
that no book can be apprec[...]ed until it has been slept with
and dreamed over. You rec[...]l, perhaps, that eloquent
passage in his noble defenc[...] of the poet Archias, wherein
Cicero (not Kikero) refers [...] his own pursuit of literary
studies: "Haec studia adole[...]entiam alunt, senectutem
oblectant; secundas res orn[...]t, adversis perfugium ac
solatium praebent; delectar[...]lomi, non impediunt foris;
PERNOCTANT nobiscum[...]eregrinantur, rusticantur!"

By the gods! you spoke tal[...] friend Cicero; for it is indeed
so, that these pursuits nour[...] our earlier and delight our
later years, dignifying the [...]nor details of life and
affording a perennial refug[...]nd solace; at home they
please us and in no vocatio[...]elsewhere do they embarrass
us; they are with us by nigl[...] they go with us upon our
travels, and even upon our [...]tirement into the country do
they accompany us!

I have italicized pernoctant [...]ecause it is that word which
demonstrates beyond all po[...]ibility of doubt that Cicero
made a practice of reading [...] bed. Why, I can almost see
him now, propped up in his[...]ouch, unrolling scroll after

scroll of his favorite literature, and enjoying it mightily, too, which enjoyment is interrupted now and then by the occasion which the noble reader takes to mutter maledictions upon the slave who has let the lamp run low of oil or has neglected to trim the wick.

"Peregrinantur?" Indeed, they do share our peregrinations, these literary pursuits do. If Thomas Hearne (of blessed memory!) were alive to-day he would tell us that he used always to take a book along with him whenever he went walking, and was wont to read it as he strolled along. On several occasions (as he tells us in his diary) he became so absorbed in his reading that he missed his way and darkness came upon him before he knew it.

I have always wondered why book-lovers have not had more to say of Hearne, for assuredly he was as glorious a collector as ever felt the divine fire glow within him. His character is exemplified in this prayer, which is preserved among other papers of his in the Bodleian Library:

"O most gracious and merciful Lord God, wonderful is Thy providence. I return all possible thanks to Thee for the care Thou hast always taken of me. I continually meet with most signal instances of this Thy providence, and one act yesterday, when I unexpectedly met with three old MSS., for which, in a particular manner, I return my thanks, beseeching Thee to continue the same protection to me, a poor, helpless sinner," etc.

Another prayer of Hearne's, illustrative of his faith in dependence upon Divine counsel, was made at the time Hearne was importuned by Dr. Bray, commissary to my Lord Bishop of London, "to go to Mary-Land" in the character of a missionary. "O Lord God, Heavenly Father, look down upon me with p...," cries this pious soul, "and be pleased to be my guide,...w I am importuned to leave the place where I have bee... ducated in the university. And of Thy great goodness I hu... ly desire Thee to signify to me what is most proper for... e to do in this affair."

Another famous man who ... de a practice of reading books as he walked the highways ... as Dr. Johnson, and it is recorded that he presented ... urious spectacle indeed, for his shortsightedness compe... d him to hold the volume close to his nose, and he sh... fled along, rather than walked, stepping high over shadow... nd stumbling over sticks and stones.

But, perhaps, the most inte...sting story illustrative of the practice of carrying one's r...ding around with one is that which is told of Professor P...rson, the Greek scholar. This human monument of learni... happened to be travelling in the same coach with a coxc...mb who sought to air his pretended learning by quot...ons from the ancients. At last old Porson asked:

"Pri'thee, sir, whence come...hat quotation?"

"From Sophocles," quoth t... vain fellow.

"Be so kind as to find it fo... e?" asked Porson, producing a copy of Sophocles from ... pocket.

Then the coxcomb, not at a... abashed, said that he meant not Sophocles, but Euripid... Whereupon Porson drew from another pocket a cop... f Euripides and challenged the upstart to find the quotatio... n question. Full of confusion, the fellow thrust his head o... of the window of the coach and cried to the driver:

"In heaven's name, put me down at once; for there is an old gentleman in here that hath the Bodleian Library in his pocket!"

Porson himself was a veritable slave to the habit of reading in bed. He would lie down with his books piled around him, then light his pipe and start in upon some favorite volume. A jug of liquor was invariably at hand, for Porson was a famous drinker. It is related that on one occasion he fell into a boosy slumber, his pipe dropped out of his mouth and set fire to the bed-clothes. But for the arrival of succor the tipsy scholar would surely have been cremated.

Another very slovenly fellow was De Quincey, and he was devoted to reading in bed. But De Quincey was a very vandal when it came to the care and use of books. He never returned volumes he borrowed, and he never hesitated to mutilate a rare book in order to save himself the labor and trouble of writing out a quotation.

But perhaps the person who did most to bring reading in bed into evil repute was Mrs. Charles Elstob, ward and sister of the Canon of Canterbury (circa 1700). In his "Dissertation on Letter-Founders," Rowe Mores describes this woman as the "indefessa comes" of her brother's studies, a female student in Oxford. She was, says Mores, a northern lady of an ancient family and a genteel fortune, "but she pursued too much the drug called learning, and in that pursuit failed of being careful of any one thing necessary. In her latter years she was tutoress in the family of the Duke of Portland, where we visited her in her sleeping-room at Bulstrode, surrounded with books and dirtiness, the usual appendages of folk of learning!"

There is another word which Cicero uses—for I have still somewhat more to say of the passage from the oration "pro Archia poeta"—the word "rusticantur," which indicates that civilization twenty centuries ago made a practice of taking books out into the country for summer reading. "These literary pursuits rusticate with us," says Cicero, and thus he presents to us a pen-picture of the Roman patrician stretched upon the cool grass under the trees, perusing the latest popular romance, while, forsooth, in yonder hammock his dignified spouse swings slowly to and fro, conning the pages and the colored plates of the current fashion journal. Surely in the telltale word "rusticantur" you and I and the rest of human nature find a worthy precedent and much encouragement for our practice of loading up with plenty of good reading before we start for the scene of our annual summering.

As for myself, I never go away from home that I do not take a trunkful of books with me, for experience has taught me that there is no companionship better than that of these friends, who, however much all things else may vary, always give the same response to my demand upon their solace and their cheer. My sister, Miss Susan, has often inveighed against this practice of mine, and it was only yesterday that she informed me that I was the most exasperating man in the world.

However, as Miss Susan's experience with men during the sixty-seven hot summers and sixty-eight hard winters of her life has been somewhat limited, I think I should bear her criticism without a murmur. Miss Susan is really one of the kindest creatures in all the world. It is her misfortune that she has had all her life an insane passion for collecting crockery, old pewter, old brass, old glass, old furniture and other trumpery of that character; a passion with which I have little sympathy. I do not know that Miss Susan is prouder of her collection of all this folderol than she is of the fact that she is a spinster.

This latter peculiarity asserts itself upon every occasion possible. I recall an unpleasant scene in the omnibus last winter, when the obsequious conductor, taking advantage of my sister's white hair and furrowed cheeks, addressed that estimable lady as "Madam." I'd have you know that my sister gave the fellow to understand very shortly and in very vigorous English (emphasized with her blue silk umbrella) that she was Miss Susan, and that she did not intend to be Madamed by anybody, under any condition.

IV

THE MANIA OF COLLECTING SEIZES ME

Captivity Waite never approved of my fondness for fairy literature. She shared the enthusiasm which I expressed whenever "Robinson Crusoe" was mentioned; there was just enough seriousness in De Foe's romance, just enough piety to appeal for sympathy to one of Captivity Waite's religious turn of mind. When it came to fiction involving witches, ogres, and flubdubs, that was too much for Captivity, and the spirit of the little Puritan revolted.

Yet I have the documentary evidence to prove that Captivity's ancestors (both paternal and maternal) were, in the palmy colonial times, a[s] [su]bject slaves to superstition as [the] Waites of Salem were famous persecutors of witches, and [Si]nai Higginbotham [(Captivity's great-great-gra[ndfather on her mother's side of the family) was Cotton Ma[the]r's boon companion, and rode around the gallows with th[at] zealous theologian on that memorable occasion when [fi]ve young women were hanged at Danvers upon the charge [o]f having tormented little children with their damnab[le] arts of witchcraft. Human thought is like a monstrous [p]endulum: it keeps swinging from one extreme to the ot[he]r. Within the compass of five generations we find the Pu[rit]an first an uncompromising believer in demonology an[d] magic, and then a scoffer at everything involving the pl[ay] of fancy.

I felt harshly toward Capti[vit]y Waite for a time, but I harbor her no ill-will now; [on] the contrary, I recall with very tender feelings the dis[tan]t time when our sympathies were the same and when w[e j]ourneyed the pathway of early youth in a companionship [san]ctified by the innocence and the loyalty and the truth of [ch]ildhood. Indeed, I am not sure that that early friendship di[d n]ot make a lasting impression upon my life; I have thoug[ht] of Captivity Waite a great many times, and I have not [i]nfrequently wondered what might have been but for th[e b]ook of fairy tales which my Uncle Cephas sent me.

She was a very pretty child [a]nd she lost none of her comeliness and none of he[r s]weetness of character as she approached maturity. I was [i]mpressed with this upon my return from college. She, to[o,] had pursued those studies deemed necessary to the ac[qu]irement of a good education; she had taken a four years' [co]urse at South Holyoke and had finished at Mrs. Willar[d's] seminary at Troy. "You will now," said her father, and [he] voiced the New England sentiment regarding young womanhood; "you will now return to the quiet of your home and under the direction of your mother study the performance of those weightier duties which qualify your sex for a realization of the solemn responsibilities of human life."

Three or four years ago a fine-looking young fellow walked in upon me with a letter of introduction from his mother. He was Captivity Waite's son! Captivity is a widow now, and she is still living in her native State, within twenty miles of the spot where she was born. Colonel Parker, her husband, left her a good property when he died, and she is famous for her charities. She has founded a village library, and she has written me on several occasions for advice upon proposed purchases of books.

I don't mind telling you that I had a good deal of malicious pleasure in sending her not long ago a reminder of old times in these words: "My valued friend," I wrote, "I see by the catalogue recently published that your village library contains, among other volumes representing the modern school of fiction, eleven copies of 'Trilby' and six copies of 'The Heavenly Twins.' I also note an absence of certain works whose influence upon my earlier life was such that I make bold to send copies of the same to your care in the hope that you will kindly present them to the library with my most cordial compliments. These are a copy each of the 'New England Primer' and Grimm's 'Household Stories.'"

At the age of twenty-three, having been graduated from college and having read the poems of Villon, the confessions of Rousseau, and Boswell's life of Johnson, I was convinced that I had comprehended the sum of human wisdom and knew all there was worth knowing. If at the present time—for I am seventy-two—I knew as much as I thought I knew at twenty-t[...]e I should undoubtedly be a prodigy of learning and wi[...]om.

I started out to be a philoso[...]er. My grandmother's death during my second year at c[...]lege possessed me of a considerable sum of money [...]nd severed every tie and sentimental obligation whi[...] had previously held me to my grandmother's wish that I b[...]ome a minister of the gospel. When I became convinced [...]at I knew everything I conceived a desire to see s[...]ething, for I had traveled none and I had met but few [...]eople.

Upon the advice of my Un[...] Cephas, I made a journey to Europe, and devoted two y[...]rs to seeing sights and to acquainting myself with th[...]eople and the customs abroad. Nine months of this time I [...]ent in Paris, which was then an irregular and unkempt c[...], but withal quite as evil as at present. I took apartments [...] the Latin Quarter, and, being of a generous nature, I dev[...]d a large share of my income to the support of certain ar[...]s and students whose talents and time were expended al[...]st exclusively in the pursuit of pleasure.

While thus serving as a vis[...]le means of support to this horde of parasites, I fell in [...]th the man who has since then been my intimate friend. J[...]e Methuen was a visitor in Paris, and we became boo[...]ompanions. It was he who rescued me from the parasi[...] and revived the flames of honorable ambition, which [...]d well-nigh been extinguished by the wretch[...] influence of Villon and Rousseau. The Judge was [...] ear my senior, and a wealthy father provided him with t[...] means for gratifying his wholesome and refined tas[...]. We two went together to London, and it was during [...]r sojourn in that capital that I began my career as a colle[...]r of books. It is simply justice to my benefactor to say that to my dear friend Methuen I am indebted for the inspiration which started me upon a course so full of sweet surprises and precious rewards.

There are very many kinds of book collectors, but I think all may be grouped in three classes, viz.: Those who collect from vanity; those who collect for the benefits of learning; those who collect through a veneration and love for books. It is not unfrequent that men who begin to collect books merely to gratify their personal vanity find themselves presently so much in love with the pursuit that they become collectors in the better sense.

Just as a man who takes pleasure in the conquest of feminine hearts invariably finds himself at last ensnared by the very passion which he has been using simply for the gratification of his vanity, I am inclined to think that the element of vanity enters, to a degree, into every phase of book collecting; vanity is, I take it, one of the essentials to a well-balanced character—not a prodigious vanity, but a prudent, well-governed one. But for vanity there would be no competition in the world; without competition there would be no progress.

In these later days I often hear this man or that sneered at because, forsooth, he collects books without knowing what the books are about. But for my part, I say that that man bids fair to be all right; he has made a proper start in the right direction, and the likelihood is that, other things being equal, he will eventually become a lover, as well as a buyer, of books. Indeed, I care not what the beginning is, so long as it be a beginning. There are different ways of reaching the goal. Some folk go horseback via the royal road, but very many others are compelled to adopt the more tedious processes, involving rocky pathways and torn shoon and sore feet.

So subtile and so infectious is this grand passion that one is hardly aware of its presence before it has complete possession of him; and I have known instances of men who, after having associated one evening with Judge Methuen and me, have waked up the next morning filled with the incurable enthusiasm of bibliomania. But the development of the passion is not always marked by exhibitions of violence; sometimes, like the measles, it is slow and obstinate about "coming out," and in such cases applications should be resorted to for the purpose of diverting the malady from the vitals; otherwise serious results may ensue.

Indeed, my learned friend Dr. O'Rell has met with several cases (as he informs me) in which suppressed bibliomania has resulted fatally. Many of these cases have been reported in that excellent publication, the "Journal of the American Medical Association," which periodical, by the way, is edited by ex-Surgeon-General Hamilton, a famous collector of the literature of ornament and dress.

To make short of a long story, the medical faculty is nearly a unit upon the proposition that wherever suppressed bibliomania is suspected intermediate steps should be taken to bring out the disease. It is true that an Ohio physician, named Woodbury, has written much in defence of the theory that bibliomania can be aborted; but a very large majority of his profession are of the opinion that the actual malady must needs run a regular course, and they insist that the cases quoted as cured by Woodbury were not genuine, but were bastard or false phases, of the same class as the chickenpox and the German measles.

My mania exhibited itself first in an affectation for old books; it mattered not what the book itself was—so long as it bore an ancient date upon its title-page or in its colophon I pined to possess it. This was not only a vanity, but a very silly one. In a month's time I had got together a large number of these old tomes, many of them folios, and nearly all badly worm-eaten, and sadly shaken.

One day I entered a shop kept by a man named Stibbs, and asked if I could procure any volumes of sixteenth-century print.

"Yes," said Mr. Stibbs, "we have a cellarful of them, and we sell them by the ton or by the cord."

That very day I dispersed my hoard of antiques, retaining only my Prynne's "Histrio-Mastix" and my Opera Quinti Horatii Flacci (8vo, Aldus, Venetiis, 1501). And then I became interested in British balladry—a noble subject, for which I have always had a veneration and love, as the well-kept and profusely annotated volumes in cases 3, 6, and 9 in the front room are ready to prove to you at any time you choose to visit my quiet, pleasant home.

V

BALDNESS AND INTELLECTUALITY

One of Judge Methuen's pet theories is that the soul in the human body lies near the center of gravity; this is, I believe, one of the tenets of the Buddhist faith, and for a long time I eschewed it as one might shun a vile thing, for I feared lest I should become identified even remotely with any faith or sect other than Congregationalism.

Yet I noticed that in moments of fear or of joy or of the sense of any other emotion I invariably experienced a feeling of goneness in the pit of my stomach, as if, forsooth, the center of my physical system were also the center of my nervous and intellectual system, the point at which were focused all those devious lines of communication by means of which sensation is instantaneously transmitted from one part of the body to another.

I mentioned this circumstance to Judge Methuen, and it seemed to please him. "My friend," said he, "you have a particularly sensitive soul; I beg of you to exercise the greatest prudence in your treatment of it. It is the best type of the bibliomaniac soul, for the quickness of its apprehensions betokens that it is alert and keen and capable of instantaneous impressions and enthusiasms. What you have just told me convinces me that you are by nature qualified for rare exploits in the science and art of book-collecting. You will presently become bald—perhaps as bald as Thomas Hobbes was—for a vigilant and active soul invariably compels baldness, so close are the relations between the soul and the brain, and so destructive are the growth and operations of the soul to those vestigial features which humanity has inherited from those grosser animals, our prehistoric ancestors."

You see by this that Judge Methuen recognized baldness as prima-facie evidence of intellectuality and spirituality. He has collected much literature upon the subject, and has promised the Academy of Science to prepare and read for the instruction of that learned body an essay demonstrating that absence of hair from the cranium (particularly from the superior regions of the frontal and parietal divisions) proves a departure from the instincts and practices of brute humanity, and indicates surely the growth of the understanding.

It occurred to the Judge long ago to prepare a list of the names of the famous bald men in the history of human society, and this list has grown until it includes the names of thousands, representing every profession and vocation. Homer, Socrates, Confucius, Aristotle, Plato, Cicero, Pliny, Maecenas, Julius Caesar, Horace, Shakespeare, Bacon, Napoleon Bonaparte, Dante, Pope, Cowper, Goldsmith, Wordsworth, Israel Putnam, John Quincy Adams, Patrick Henry—these geniuses all were bald. But the baldest of all was the philosopher Hobbes, of whom the revered John Aubrey has recorded that "he was very bald, yet within dore he used to study and sitt bare-headed, and said he never took cold in his head, but that the greatest trouble was to keepe off the flies from pitching on the baldness."

In all the portraits and pictures of Bonaparte which I have seen, a conspicuous feature is that curl or lock of hair which depends upon the emperor's forehead, and gives to the face a pleasant degree of picturesque distinction. Yet this was a vanity, and really a laughable one; for early in life Bonaparte began to get bald, and this so troubled him that he sought to overcome the change it made in his appearance by growing a long strand of hair upon his occiput and bringing it forward a goodly distance in such artful wise that it right ingeniously served the purposes of that Hyperion curl which had been the pride of his youth, but which had fallen early before the ravages of time.

As for myself, I do not know that I ever shared that derisive opinion in which the unthinking are wont to hold baldness. Nay, on the contrary, I have always had especial reverence for this mark of intellectuality, and I agree with my friend Judge Methuen that the tragic episode recorded in the second chapter of II. Kings should serve the honorable purpose of indicating to humanity that bald heads are favored with the approval and the protection of Divinity.

In my own case I have imputed my early baldness to growth in intellectuality and spirituality induced by my fondness for and devotion to books. Miss Susan, my sister, lays it to other causes, first among which she declares to be my unnatural practice of reading in bed, and the second my habit of eating welsh-rarebits late of nights. Over my bed I have a gas-jet so properly shaded that the rays of light are concentrated and reflected downward upon the volume which I am reading.

Miss Susan insists that much of this light and its attendant heat falls upon my head, compelling there a dryness of the scalp whereby the follicles have been deprived of their natural nourishment and have consequently died. She furthermore maintains that the welsh-rarebits of which I partake invariably at the eleventh hour every night breed poisonous vapors and subtle megrims within my stomach, which humors, rising by their natural courses to my brain, do therein produce a fever that from within burneth up the fluids necessary to a healthy condition of the capillary growth upon the super-adjacent and exterior cranial integument.

Now, this very declaration of Miss Susan's gives me a potent argument in defence of my practices, for, being bald, would not a neglect of those means whereby warmth is engendered where it is needed result in colds, quinsies, asthmas, and a thousand other banes? The same benignant Providence which, according to Laurence Sterne, tempereth the wind to the shorn lamb provideth defence and protection for the bald. Had I not loved books, the soul in my midriff had not done away with those capillary vestiges of my simian ancestry which originally flourished upon my scalp; had I not become bald, the delights and profits of reading in bed might never have fallen to my lot.

And indeed baldness has its compensations; when I look about me and see the time, the energy, and the money that are continually expended upon the nurture and tending of the hair, I am thankful that my lot is what it is. For now my money is applied to the buying of books, and my time and energy are devoted to the reading of them.

To thy vain employments, thou becurled and pomaded Absalom! Sweeter than thy unguents and cosmetics and Sabean perfumes is the smell of those old books of mine, which from the years and from the ship's hold and from constant companionship with sages and philosophers have acquired a fragrance that exalteth the soul and quickeneth the intellectuals! Let me paraphrase my dear Chaucer and tell thee, thou waster of substances, that

For me was lever han at m… eddes hed

A twenty bokes, clothed in … ack and red

Of Aristotle and his philos… hie,

Than robes rich, or fidel, o… autrie;

But all be that I ben a phil… pher

Yet have I but litel gold in … fre!

Books, books, books—giv… ne ever more books, for they are the caskets wherein we … nd the immortal expressions of humanity—words, the onl… ings that live forever! I bow reverently to the bust in yo… er corner whenever I recall what Sir John Herschel (G… rest his dear soul!) said and wrote: "Were I to pay for a … ste that should stand me in stead under every variety o… ircumstances and be a source of happiness and cheerfuln… s to me during life, and a shield against its ills, howe… r things might go amiss and the world frown upon me, … vould be a taste for reading. Give a man this taste and a … eans of gratifying it, and you can hardly fail of making h… n a happy man; unless, indeed, you put into his hands a m… perverse selection of books. You place him in contact v… h the best society in every period of history—with the … /isest, the wittiest, the tenderest, the bravest, and … e purest characters who have adorned humanity. You ma… e him a denizen of all nations, a contemporary of all ages… he world has been created for him."

For one phrase particularly … o all good men, methinks, bless burly, bearish, phrase… aaking old Tom Carlyle. "Of all things," quoth he, "which men do or make here below by far the most momentous, wonderful, and worthy are the things we call books." And Judge Methuen's favorite quotation is from Babington Macaulay to this effect: "I would rather be a poor man in a garret with plenty of books than a king who did not love reading."

Kings, indeed! What a sorry lot are they! Said George III. to Nicol, his bookseller: "I would give this right hand if the same attention had been paid to my education which I pay to that of the prince." Louis XIV. was as illiterate as the lowliest hedger and ditcher. He could hardly write his name; at first, as Samuel Pegge tells us, he formed it out of six straight strokes and a line of beauty, thus:

I I I I I I S

—which he afterward perfected as best he could, and the result was LOUIS.

Still I find it hard to inveigh against kings when I recall the goodness of Alexander to Aristotle, for without Alexander we should hardly have known of Aristotle. His royal patron provided the philosopher with every advantage for the acquisition of learning, dispatching couriers to all parts of the earth to gather books and manuscripts and every variety of curious thing likely to swell the store of Aristotle's knowledge.

Yet set them up in a line and survey them—these wearers of crowns and these wielders of scepters—and how pitiable are they in the paucity and vanity of their accomplishments! What knew they of the true happiness of human life? They and their courtiers are dust and forgotten.

Judge Methuen and I shall in due time pass away, but our courtiers—they who have ever contributed to our delight and solace—our Horace, our Cervantes, our Shakespeare, and the rest of the innumerable train—these shall never die. And inspired and sustained by this immortal companionship we blithely walk the pathway illumined by its glory, and we sing, in season and out, the song ever dear to us and ever dear to thee, we hope, O gentle reader:

Oh, for a booke and a shady nooke,

Eyther in doore or out,

With the greene leaves whispering overhead,

Or the streete cryes all about

Where I maie reade all at my ease

Both of the newe and old,

For a jollie goode booke whereon to looke

Is better to me than golde!

VI

MY ROMANCE WITH FIAMMETTA

My bookseller and I came nigh to blows some months ago over an edition of Boccaccio, which my bookseller tried to sell me. This was a copy in the original, published at Antwerp in 1603, prettily rubricated, and elaborately adorned with some forty or fifty copperplates illustrative of the text. I dare say the volume was cheap enough at thirty dollars, but I did not want it.

My reason for not wanting it gave rise to that discussion between my bookseller and myself, which became very heated before it ended. I said very frankly that I did not care for the book in the original, because I had several translations done by the most competent hands. Thereupon my bookseller ventured that aged and hackneyed argument which has for centuries done the book trade such effective service—namely, that in every translation, no matter how good that translation may be, there is certain to be lost a share of the flavor and spirit of the meaning.

"Fiddledeedee!" said I. "Do you suppose that these translators who have devoted their lives to the study and practice of the art are not competent to interpret the different shades and colors of meaning better than the mere dabbler in foreign tongues? And then, again, is not human life too short for the lover of books to spend his precious time digging out the recondite allusions of authors, lexicon in hand? My dear sir, it is a wickedly false economy to expend time and money for that which one can get done much better and at a much [sm]aller expenditure by another hand."

From my encounter with m[y] bookseller I went straight home and took down my fa[vo]rite copy of the "Decameron" and thumbed it over very t[ender]ly; for you must know that I am particularly attached to [th]at little volume. I can hardly realize that nearly half a ce[nt]ury has elapsed since Yseult Hardynge and I parted. She [w]as such a creature as the great novelist himself would hav[e c]hosen for a heroine; she had the beauty and the wit of th[os]e Florentine ladies who flourished in the fourteenth [c]entury, and whose graces of body and mind have been i[m]mortalized by Boccaccio. Her eyes, as I particularly recal[l,] were specially fine, reflecting from their dark depths ever[y] expression of her varying moods.

Why I called her Fiammett[a I] cannot say, for I do not remember; perhaps from a [bo]yish fancy, merely. At that time Boccaccio and I were [fa]mous friends; we were together constantly, and his [c]ompanionship had such an influence upon me that for [th]e nonce I lived and walked and had my being in that di[st]ant, romantic period when all men were gallants and all [wo]men were grandes dames and all birds were nightingales.

I bought myself an old Flor[en]tine sword at Noseda's in the Strand and hung it on the w[al]l in my modest apartments; under it I placed Boccaccio['s] portrait and Fiammetta's, and I was wont to drink toasts t[o t]hese beloved counterfeit presentments in flagons (m[in]d you, genuine antique flagons) of Italian wine. Tw[ic]e I took Fiammetta boating upon the Thames and once [to] view the Lord Mayor's pageant; her mother was w[ith] us on both occasions, but she might as well have been at [th]e bottom of the sea, for she was a stupid old soul, wholly incapable of sharing or appreciating the poetic enthusiasms of romantic youth.

Had Fiammetta been a book—ah, unfortunate lady!—had she but been a book she might still be mine, for me to care for lovingly and to hide from profane eyes and to attire in crushed levant and gold and to cherish as a best-beloved companion in mine age! Had she been a book she could not have been guilty of the folly of wedding with a yeoman of Lincolnshire—ah me, what rude awakenings too often dispel the pleasing dreams of youth!

When I revisited England in the sixties, I was tempted to make an excursion into Lincolnshire for the purpose of renewing my acquaintance with Fiammetta. Before, however, I had achieved that object this thought occurred to me: "You are upon a fool's errand; turn back, or you will destroy forever one of the sweetest of your boyhood illusions! You seek Fiammetta in the delusive hope of finding her in the person of Mrs. Henry Boggs; there is but one Fiammetta, and she is the memory abiding in your heart. Spare yourself the misery of discovering in the hearty, fleshy Lincolnshire hussif the decay of the promises of years ago; be content to do reverence to the ideal Fiammetta who has built her little shrine in your sympathetic heart!"

Now this was strange counsel, yet it had so great weight with me that I was persuaded by it, and after lying a night at the Swan-and-Quiver Tavern I went back to London, and never again had a desire to visit Lincolnshire.

But Fiammetta is still a pleasing memory—ay, and more than a memory to me, for whenever I take down that precious book and open it, what a host of friends do troop forth! Cavaliers, princesses, courtiers, damoiselles, monks, nuns, equerries, pages, maidens—humanity of every class and condition, and all instinct with the color of the master magician, Boccaccio!

And before them all cometh a maiden with dark, glorious eyes, and she beareth garlands of roses; the moonlight falleth like a benediction upon the Florentine garden slope, and the night wind seeketh its cradle in the laurel tree, and fain would sleep to the song of the nightingale.

As for Judge Methuen, he loves his Boccaccio quite as much as I do mine, and being somewhat of a versifier he has made a little poem on the subject, a copy of which I have secured surreptitiously and do now offer for your delectation:

One day upon a topmost shelf

I found a precious prize indeed,

Which father used to read himself,

But did not want us boys to read;

A brown old book of certain age

(As type and binding seemed to show),

While on the spotted title-page

Appeared the name "Boccaccio."

I'd never heard that name before,

But in due season it became

To him who fondly brooded o'er

Those pages a beloved name!

Adown the centuries I walked

Mid pastoral scenes and royal show;

With seigneurs and their dames I talked—

The crony of Boccaccio!

Those courtly knights and sprightly maids,

Who really seemed disposed to shine

In gallantries and escapades,

Anon became great friends of mine.

Yet was there sentiment with fun,

And oftentimes my tears would flow

At some quaint tale of valor done,

As told by my Boccaccio.

In boyish dreams I saw again

Bucolic belles and dames of court,

The princely youths and monkish men

Arrayed for sacrifice or sport.

Again I heard the nightingale

Sing as she sang those years ago

In his embowered Italian vale

To my revered Boccaccio.

And still I love that brown old book

I found upon the topmost shelf—

I love it so I let none look

Upon the treasure but myself!

And yet I have a strapping boy

Who (I have every cause to know)

Would to its full extent enjoy

The friendship of Boccaccio.

But boys are, oh! so different now

From what they were when I was one!

I fear my boy would not know how

To take that old raconteur's fun!

In your companionship, O friend,

I think it wise alone to go

Plucking the gracious fruits that bend

Wheree'er you lead, Boccaccio.

So rest you there upon the shelf,

Clad in your garb of faded brown;

Perhaps, sometime, my boy himself

Shall find you out and take you down.

Then may he feel the joy once more

That thrilled me, filled me years ago

When reverently I brooded o'er

The glories of Boccaccio!

Out upon the vile brood of [...] itators, I say! Get ye gone, ye
Bandellos and ye Straparol [...] and ye other charlatans who
would fain possess yoursel [...] s of the empire which the
genius of Boccaccio beque [...] ed to humanity. There is but
one master, and to him we [...] der grateful homage. He
leads us down through the [...] isters of time, and at his
touch the dead become rea [...] nate, and all the sweetness
and the valor of antiquity r [...] ur; heroism, love, sacrifice,
tears, laughter, wisdom, wi [...] philosophy, charity, and
understanding are his auxil [...] ies; humanity is his
inspiration, humanity his th [...] ne, humanity his audience,
humanity his debtor.

Now it is of Tancred's daug [...] ter he tells, and now of
Rossiglione's wife; anon of [...] e cozening gardener he
speaks and anon of Alibec [...] of what befell Gillette de
Narbonne, of Iphigenia and [...] ymon, of Saladin, of
Calandrino, of Dianora and [...] nsaldo we hear; and what
subject soever he touches h [...] quickens it into life, and he so
subtly invests it with that i [...] efinable quality of his genius
as to attract thereunto not o [...] y our sympathies but also our
enthusiasm.

Yes, truly, he should be rea [...] with understanding; what
author should not? I would [...] o more think of putting my
Boccaccio into the hands o [...] dullard than I would think of
leaving a bright and beauti [...] woman at the mercy of a
blind mute.

I have hinted at the horror [...] the fate which befell Yseult
Hardynge in the seclusion [...] Mr. Henry Boggs's
Lincolnshire estate. Mr. H [...] y Boggs knew nothing of
romance, and he cared less [...] e was wholly incapable of
appreciating a woman with [...] ark, glorious eyes and an
expanding soul; I'll warran [...] e that he would at any time

gladly have traded a "Decameron" for a copy of "The Gentleman Poulterer," or for a year's subscription to that grewsome monument to human imbecility, London "Punch."

Ah, Yseult! hadst thou but been a book!

VII

THE DELIGHTS OF FENDER-FISHING

I should like to have met Izaak Walton. He is one of the few authors whom I know I should like to have met. For he was a wise man, and he had understanding. I should like to have gone angling with him, for I doubt not that like myself he was more of an angler theoretically than practically. My bookseller is a famous fisherman, as, indeed, booksellers generally are, since the methods employed by fishermen to deceive and to catch their finny prey are very similar to those employed by booksellers to attract and to entrap buyers.

As for myself, I regard angling as one of the best of avocations, and although I have pursued it but little, I concede that doubtless had I practised it oftener I should have been a better man. How truly has Dame Juliana Berners said that "at the least the angler hath his wholesome walk and merry at his ease, and a sweet air of

51

the sweet savour of the meadow flowers that maketh him hungry; he heareth the melodious harmony of fowls; he seeth the young swans, herons, ducks, cotes, and many other fowls with their broods, which meseemeth better than all the noise of hounds, the blasts of horns, and the cry of fowls that hunters, falconers and fowlers can make. And IF the angler take fish—surely then is there no man merrier than he is in his spirit!"

My bookseller cannot understand how it is that, being so enthusiastic a fisherman theoretically, I should at the same time indulge so seldom in the practice of fishing, as if, forsooth, a man should be expected to engage continually and actively in every art and practice of which he may happen to approve. My young friend Edward Ayer has a noble collection of books relating to the history of American aboriginals and of the wars waged between those Indians and the settlers in this country; my other young friend Luther Mills has gathered together a multitude of books treating of the Napoleonic wars; yet neither Ayer nor Mills hath ever slain a man or fought a battle, albeit both find delectation in recitals of warlike prowess and personal valor. I love the night and the poetic influences of that quiet time, but I do not sit up all night in order to hear the nightingale or to contemplate the astounding glories of the heavens.

For similar reasons, much as I appreciate and marvel at the beauties of early morning, I do not make a practice of early rising, and sensible as I am to the charms of the babbling brook and of the crystal lake, I am not addicted to the practice of wading about in either to the danger either to my own health or to the health of the finny denizens in those places.

The best anglers in the world are those who do not catch fish; the mere slaughter of fish is simply brutal, and it was with a view to keeping her excellent treatise out of the hands of the idle and the inappreciative that Dame Berners incorporated that treatise in a compendious book whose cost was so large that only "gentyll and noble men" could possess it. What mind has he who loveth fishing merely for the killing it involves—what mind has such a one to the beauty of the ever-changing panorama which nature unfolds to the appreciative eye, or what communion has he with those sweet and uplifting influences in which the meadows, the hillsides, the glades, the dells, the forests, and the marshes abound?

Out upon these vandals, I say—out upon the barbarians who would rob angling of its poesy, and reduce it to the level of the butcher's trade! It becomes a base and vicious avocation, does angling, when it ceases to be what Sir Henry Wotton loved to call it—"an employment for his idle time, which was then not idly spent; a rest to his mind, a cheerer of his spirits, a diverter of sadness, a calmer of unquiet thoughts, a moderator of passions, a procurer of contentedness, and a begetter of habits of peace and patience in those that professed and practised it!"

There was another man I should like to have met—Sir Henry Wotton; for he was an ideal angler. Christopher North, too ("an excellent angler and now with God"!)—how I should love to have explored the Yarrow with him, for he was a man of vast soul, vast learning, and vast wit.

"Would you believe it, my dear Shepherd," said he, "that my piscatory passions are almost dead within me, and I like now to saunter along the banks and braes, eying the younkers angling, or to lay me down on some sunny spot, and with my face up to heaven, watch the slow-changing clouds!"

THERE was the angling genius with whom I would fain go angling!

"Angling," says our revered St. Izaak, "angling is somewhat like poetry—men are to be born so."

Doubtless there are poets who are not anglers, but doubtless there never was an angler who was not also a poet. Christopher North was a famous fisherman; he began his career as such when he was a child of three years. With his thread line and bent-pin hook the wee tot set out to make his first cast in "a wee burnie" he had discovered near his home. He caught his fish, too, and for the rest of the day he carried the miserable little specimen about on a plate, exhibiting it triumphantly. With that first experience began a life which I am fain to regard as one glorious song in praise of the beauty and the beneficence of nature.

My bookseller once took me angling with him in a Wisconsin lake which was the property of a club of anglers to which my friend belonged. As we were to be absent several days I carried along a box of books, for I esteem appropriate reading to be a most important adjunct to an angling expedition. My bookseller had with him enough machinery to stock a whaling expedition, and I could not help wondering what my old Walton would think, could he drop down into our company with his modest equipment of hooks, flies, and gentles.

The lake whither we went was a large and beautiful expanse, girt by a landscape which to my fancy was the embodiment of poetic delicacy and suggestion. I began to inquire about the chub, dace, and trouts, but my bookseller lost no time in telling me that the lake had been rid of all cheap fry, and had been stocked with game fish, such as bass and pike.

I did not at all relish this covert sneer at traditions which I have always reverenced, and the better acquainted I became with my bookseller's modern art of angling the less I liked it. I have little love for that kind of angling which does not admit of a simultaneous enjoyment of the surrounding beauties of nature. My bookseller enjoined silence upon me, but I did not heed the injunction, for I must, indeed, have been a mere wooden effigy to hold my peace amid that picturesque environment of hill, valley, wood, meadow, and arching sky of clear blue.

It was fortunate for me that I had my "Noctes Ambrosianae" along, for when I had exhausted my praise of the surrounding glories of nature, my bookseller would not converse with me; so I opened my book and read to him that famous passage between Kit North and the Ettrick Shepherd, wherein the shepherd discourses boastfully of his prowess as a piscator of sawmon.

As the sun approached midheaven and its heat became insupportable, I raised my umbrella; to this sensible proceeding my bookseller objected—in fact, there was hardly any reasonable suggestion I had to make for beguiling the time that my bookseller did not protest against it, and when finally I produced my "Newcastle Fisher's Garlands" from my basket, and began to troll those spirited lines beginning

Away wi' carking care and [...] oom

That make life's pathway w[...] dy O!

A cheerful glass makes flo[...] rs to bloom

And lightsome hours fly sp[...] dy O!

he gathered in his rod and t[...] kle, and declared that it was
no use trying to catch fish [...] ile Bedlam ran riot.

As for me, I had a delightf[...] time of it; I caught no fish, to
be sure: but what of that? I [...] OULD have caught fish had I
so desired, but, as I have al[...] ady intimated to you and as I
have always maintained an[...] lways shall, the mere
catching of fish is the least [...] the many enjoyments
comprehended in the broa[...] racious art of angling.

Even my bookseller was c[...] pelled to admit ultimately that
I was a worthy disciple of [...] alton, for when we had
returned to the club house [...] d had partaken of our supper I
regaled the company with [...] ny a cheery tale and merry
song which I had gathered [...] m my books. Indeed, before I
returned to the city I was e[...] ted an honorary member of
the club by acclamation—[...] for the number of fish I had
expiscated (for I did not ca[...] one), but for that mastery of
the science of angling and [...] literature and the traditions
and the religion and the ph[...] sophy thereof which, by the
grace of the companionshi[...] f books, I had achieved.

It is said that, with his feet [...] er the fender, Macaulay could
discourse learnedly of Fren[...] poetry, art, and philosophy.
Yet he never visited Paris t[...] t he did not experience the

most exasperating difficulties in making himself understood by the French customs officers.

In like manner I am a fender-fisherman. With my shins toasting before a roaring fire, and with Judge Methuen at my side, I love to exploit the joys and the glories of angling. The Judge is "a brother of the angle," as all will allow who have heard him tell Father Prout's story of the bishop and the turbots or heard him sing—

With angle rod and lightsome heart,

Our conscience clear, we gay depart

To pebbly brooks and purling streams,

And ne'er a care to vex our dreams.

And how could the lot of the fender-fisherman be happier? No colds, quinsies or asthmas follow his incursions into the realms of fancy where in cool streams and peaceful lakes a legion of chubs and trouts and sawmon await him; in fancy he can hie away to the far-off Yalrow and once more share the benefits of the companionship of Kit North, the Shepherd, and that noble Edinburgh band; in fancy he can trudge the banks of the Blackwater with the sage of Watergrasshill; in fancy he can hear the music of the Tyne and feel the wind sweep cool and fresh o'er Coquetdale; in fancy, too, he knows the friendships which only he can know—the friendships of the immortals whose spirits hover where human love and sympathy attract them.

How well I love ye, O my [...]cious books—my Prout, my
Wilson, my Phillips, my B[...]ers, my Doubleday, my
Roxby, my Chatto, my Tho[...]pson, my Crawhall! For ye are
full of joyousness and chee[...] and your songs uplift me and
make me young and strong [...]ain.

And thou, homely little bro[...]n thing with worn leaves, yet
more precious to me than a[...] jewels of the earth—come, let
me take thee from thy shel[...]nd hold thee lovingly in my
hands and press thee tende[...] to this aged and slow-pulsing
heart of mine! Dost thou re[...]ember how I found thee half a
century ago all tumbled in [...]ot of paltry trash? Did I not
joyously possess thee for a [...]xpence, and have I not
cherished thee full sweetly [...]l these years? My Walton,
soon must we part forever; [...]hen I am gone say unto him
who next shall have thee to [...]is own that with his latest
breath an old man blessed t[...]e!

VIII

BALLADS AND THEIR MAKERS

One of the most interesting spots in all London to me is Bunhill Fields cemetery, for herein are the graves of many whose memory I revere. I had heard that Joseph Ritson was buried here, and while my sister, Miss Susan, lingered at the grave of her favorite poet, I took occasion to spy around among the tombstones in the hope of discovering the last resting-place of the curious old antiquary whose labors in the field of balladry have placed me under so great a debt of gratitude to him.

But after I had searched in vain for somewhat more than an hour one of the keepers of the place told me that in compliance with Ritson's earnest desire while living, that antiquary's grave was immediately after the interment of the body levelled down and left to the care of nature, with no stone to designate its location. So at the present time no one knows just where old Ritson's grave is, only that within that vast enclosure where so many thousand souls sleep their last sleep the dust of the famous ballad-lover lies fast asleep in the bosom of mother earth.

I have never been able to awaken in Miss Susan any enthusiasm for balladry. My worthy sister is of a serious turn of mind, and I have heard her say a thousand times that convivial songs (which is her name for balladry) are inspirations, if not actually compositions, of the devil. In her younger days Miss Susan performed upon the melodeon with much discretion, and at one time I indulged the delusive hope that eventually she would not disdain to join me in the vocal performance of the best ditties of D'Urfey and his ilk.

If I do say it myself, I had a very pretty voice thirty or forty years ago, and even at the present time I can deliver the ballad of King Cophetua and the beggar maid with amazing spirit when I have my friend Judge Methuen at my side and a bowl of steaming punch between us. But my education of Miss Susan ended without being finished. We two learned to perform the ballad of Sir Patrick Spens very acceptably, but Miss Susan abandoned the copartnership when I insisted that we proceed to the sprightly ditty beginning,

Life's short hours too fast are hasting—

Sweet amours cannot be lasting.

My physician, Dr. O'Rell, has often told me that he who has a well-assorted ballad library should never be lonely, for the limitations of ballads are so broad that within them are to be found performances adapted to every mood to which humanity is liable. And, indeed, my experience confirms the truth of my physician's theory. It were hard for me to tell what delight I have had upon a hot and gusty day in a perusal of the history of Robin Hood, for there is such actuality in those simple rhymes as to dispel the troublesome environments of the present and transport me to better times and pleasanter scenes.

Aha! how many times have I walked with brave Robin in Sherwood forest! How many times have Little John and I couched under the greenwood tree and shared with Friar Tuck the haunch of juicy venison and the pottle of brown

October brew! And Will Scarlet and I have been famous friends these many a year, and if Allen-a-Dale were here he would tell you that I have trolled full many a ballad with him in praise of Maid Marian's peerless beauty.

Who says that Sherwood is no more and that Robin and his merry men are gone forever! Why, only yesternight I walked with them in that gracious forest and laughed defiance at the doughty sheriff and his craven menials. The moonlight twinkled and sifted through the boscage, and the wind was fresh and cool. Right merrily we sang, and I doubt not we should have sung the whole night through had not my sister, Miss Susan, come tapping at my door, saying that I had waked her parrot and would do well to cease my uproar and go to sleep.

Judge Methuen has a copy of Bishop Percy's "Reliques of Ancient English Poetry" that he prizes highly. It is the first edition of this noble work, and was originally presented by Percy to Dr. Birch of the British Museum. The Judge found these three volumes exposed for sale in a London book stall, and he comprehended them without delay—a great bargain, you will admit, when I tell you that they cost the Judge but three shillings! How came these precious volumes into that book stall I shall not presume to say.

Strange indeed are the vicissitudes which befall books, stranger even than the happenings in human life. All men are not as considerate of books as I am; I wish they were. Many times I have felt the deepest compassion for noble volumes in the possession of persons wholly incapable of appreciating them. The helpless books seemed to appeal to me to rescue them, and too many times I have been tempted to snatch them from their inhospitable shelves, and march them away to a pleasant refuge beneath my own comfortable roof tree.

Too few people seem to realize that books have feelings. But if I know one thing better than another I know this, that my books know me and love me. When of a morning I awaken I cast my eyes about my room to see how fare my beloved treasures, and as I say cheerily to them, "Good-day to you, sweet friends!" how lovingly they beam upon me, and how glad they are that my repose has been unbroken. When I take them from their places, how tenderly do they respond to the caresses of my hands, and with what exultation do they respond unto my call for sympathy!

Laughter for my gayer moods, distraction for my cares, solace for my griefs, gossip for my idler moments, tears for my sorrows, counsel for my doubts, and assurance against my fears—these things my books give me with a promptness and a certainty and a cheerfulness which are more than human; so that I were less than human did I not love these comforters and bear eternal gratitude to them.

Judge Methuen read me once a little poem which I fancy mightily; it is entitled "Winifreda," and you will find it in your Percy, if you have one. The last stanza, as I recall it, runs in this wise:

And when by envy time transported

Shall seek to rob us of our joys,

You'll in our girls again be courted

And I'll go wooing in our boys.

"Now who was the author of those lines?" asked the Judge.

"Undoubtedly Oliver Wendell Holmes," said I. "They have the flavor peculiar to our Autocrat; none but he could have done up so much sweetness in such a quaint little bundle."

"You are wrong," said the Judge, "but the mistake is a natural one. The whole poem is such a one as Holmes might have written, but it saw the light long before our dear doctor's day: what a pity that its authorship is not known!"

"Yet why a pity?" quoth I. "Is it not true that words are the only things that live forever? Are we not mortal, and are not books immortal? Homer's harp is broken and Horace's lyre is unstrung, and the voices of the great singers are hushed; but their songs—their songs are imperishable. O friend! what moots it to them or to us who gave this epic or that lyric to immortality? The singer belongs to a year, his song to all time. I know it is the custom now to credit the author with his work, for this is a utilitarian age, and all things are by the pound or the piece, and for so much money.

"So when a song is printed it is printed in small type, and the name of him who wrote it is appended thereunto in big type. If the song be meritorious it goes to the corners of the earth through the medium of the art preservative of arts, but the longer and the farther it travels the bigger does the type of the song become and the smaller becomes the type wherein the author's name is set.

"Then, finally, some inconsiderate hand, wielding the pen or shears, blots out or snips off the poet's name, and henceforth the song is anonymous. A great iconoclast—a royal old iconoclast—is Time: but he hath no terrors for

those precious things whic[...]re embalmed in words, and
the only fellow that shall s[...]ly escape him till the crack of
doom is he whom men kno[...] by the name of Anonymous!"

"Doubtless you speak truly[...] said the Judge; "yet it would
be different if I but had the [...]dering of things. I would let
the poets live forever and I [...]ould kill off most of their
poetry."

I do not wonder that Ritso[...]nd Percy quarrelled. It was his
misfortune that Ritson qua[...]lled with everybody. Yet
Ritson was a scrupulously [...]nest man; he was so vulgarly
sturdy in his honesty that h[...]vould make all folk tell the
truth even though the truth [...]ere of such a character as to
bring the blush of shame to[...]ie devil's hardened cheek.

On the other hand, Percy b[...]eved that there were certain
true things which should n[...] be opened out in the broad
light of day; it was this dee[...] seated conviction which kept
him from publishing the m[...]uscript folio, a priceless
treasure, which Ritson nev[...] saw and which, had it fallen in
Ritson's way instead of Per[...]'s, would have been clapped at
once into the hands of the [...]nter.

How fortunate it is for us t[...]t we have in our time so great
a scholar as Francis James [...]ild, so enamored of balladry
and so learned in it, to com[...]ete and finish the work of his
predecessors. I count myse[...]happy that I have heard from
the lips of this enthusiast s[...]eral of the rarest and noblest
of the old British and old S[...]ttish ballads; and I recall with
pride that he complimente[...]ie upon my spirited vocal
rendering of "Burd Isabel a[...]l Sir Patrick," "Lang Johnny
More," "The Duke o' Gord[...]'s Daughter," and two or three
other famous songs which [...]ad learned while sojourning
among the humbler classes [...] the North of England.

After paying our compliments to the Robin Hood garlands, to Scott, to Kirkpatrick Sharpe, to Ritson, to Buchan, to Motherwell, to Laing, to Christie, to Jamieson, and to the other famous lovers and compilers of balladry, we fell to discoursing of French song and of the service that Francis Mahony performed for English-speaking humanity when he exploited in his inimitable style those lyrics of the French and the Italian people which are now ours as much as they are anybody else's.

Dear old Beranger! what wonder that Prout loved him, and what wonder that we all love him? I have thirty odd editions of his works, and I would walk farther to pick up a volume of his lyrics than I would walk to secure any other book, excepting of course a Horace. Beranger and I are old cronies. I have for the great master a particularly tender feeling, and all on account of Fanchonette.

But there—you know nothing of Fanchonette, because I have not told you of her. She, too, should have been a book instead of the dainty, coquettish Gallic maiden that she was.

X

BOOKSELLERS AND PRINTERS, OLD AND NEW

Judge Methuen tells me that he fears what I have said about my bookseller will create the impression that I am unkindly disposed toward the bookselling craft. For the last fifty years I have had uninterrupted dealings with booksellers, and none knows better than the booksellers themselves that I particularly admire them as a class. Visitors to my home have noticed that upon my walls are hung noble portraits of Caxton, Wynkin de Worde, Richard Pynson, John Wygthe, Rayne Wolfe, John Daye, Jacob Tonson, Richard Johnes, John Dunton, and other famous old printers and booksellers.

I have, too, a large collection of portraits of modern booksellers, including a pen-and-ink sketch of Quaritch, a line engraving of Rimell, and a very excellent etching of my dear friend, the late Henry Stevens. One of the portraits is a unique, for I had it painted myself, and I have never permitted any copy to be made of it; it is of my bookseller, and it represents him in the garb of a fisherman, holding his rod and reel in one hand and the copy of the "Compleat Angler" in the other.

Mr. Curwen speaks of booksellers as being "singularly thrifty, able, industrious, and persevering—in some few cases singularly venturesome, liberal, and kind-hearted." My own observation and experience have taught me that as a class booksellers are exceptionally intelligent, ranking with printers in respect to the variety and extent of their learning.

They have, however, this distinct advantage over the printers—they are not brought in contact with the manifold temptations to intemperance and profligacy which environ the votaries of the art preservative of arts. Horace Smith has said that "were there no readers there certainly would be no writers; clearly, therefore, the existence of writers depends upon the existence of readers: and, of course, since the cause must be antecedent to the effect, readers existed before writers. Yet, on the other hand, if there were no writers there could be no readers; so it would appear that writers must be antecedent to readers."

It amazes me that a reasoner so shrewd, so clear, and so exacting as Horace Smith did not pursue the proposition further; for without booksellers there would have been no market for books—the author would not have been able to sell, and the reader would not have been able to buy.

The further we proceed with the investigation the more satisfied we become that the original man was three of number, one of him being the bookseller, who established friendly relations between the other two of him, saying: "I will serve you both by inciting both a demand and a supply." So then the author did his part, and the reader his, which I take to be a much more dignified scheme than that suggested by Darwin and his school of investigators.

By the very nature of their occupation booksellers are broad-minded; their association with every class of humanity and their constant companionship with books give them a liberality that enables them to view with singular clearness and dispassionateness every phase of life and every dispensation of Providence. They are not always practical, for the development of the spiritual and intellectual natures in man does not at the same time promote dexterity in the us...)f the baser organs of the body, I have known philos... hers who could not harness a horse or even shoo chicken...

Ralph Waldo Emerson onc... :onsumed several hours' time trying to determine whethe... ιe should trundle a wheelbarrow by pushing it... by pulling it. A. Bronson Alcott once tried to constru... a chicken coop, and he had boarded himself up inside t... structure before he discovered that he had not... ovided for a door or for windows. We have all hear... the story of Isaac Newton— how he cut two holes in his... tudy-door, a large one for his cat to enter by, and a small... ιe for the kitten.

This unworldliness—this i... ossibility, if you please—is characteristic of intellectua... orogression. Judge Methuen's second son is named Groli... and the fact that he doesn't know enough to come in o... of the rain has inspired both the Judge and myself with... e conviction that in due time Grolier will become a grea... hilosopher.

The mention of this revere... ιame reminds me that my bookseller told me the othe... lay that just before I entered his shop a wealthy patron c... he arts and muses called with a volume which he wished... have rebound.

"I can send it to Paris or to... ondon," said my bookseller. "If you have no choice of b... der, I will entrust it to Zaehnsdorf with instructio... to lavish his choicest art upon it."

"But indeed I HAVE a cho... ," cried the plutocrat, proudly. "I noticed a large number c... Grolier bindings at the Art Institute last week, and I w... t something of the same kind myself. Send the book to G... lier, and tell him to do his prettiest by it, for I can stand the expense, no matter what it is."

Somewhere in his admirable discourse old Walton has stated the theory that an angler must be born and then made. I have always held the same to be true of the bookseller. There are many, too many, charlatans in the trade; the simon-pure bookseller enters upon and conducts bookselling not merely as a trade and for the purpose of amassing riches, but because he loves books and because he has pleasure in diffusing their gracious influences.

Judge Methuen tells me that it is no longer the fashion to refer to persons or things as being "simon-pure"; the fashion, as he says, passed out some years ago when a writer in a German paper "was led into an amusing blunder by an English review. The reviewer, having occasion to draw a distinction between George and Robert Cruikshank, spoke of the former as the real Simon Pure. The German, not understanding the allusion, gravely told his readers that George Cruikshank was a pseudonym, the author's real name being Simon Pure."

This incident is given in Henry B. Wheatley's "Literary Blunders," a very charming book, but one that could have been made more interesting to me had it recorded the curious blunder which Frederick Saunders makes in his "Story of Some Famous Books." On page 169 we find this information: "Among earlier American bards we instance Dana, whose imaginative poem 'The Culprit Fay,' so replete with poetic beauty, is a fairy tale of the highlands of the Hudson. The origin of the poem is traced to a conversation with Cooper, the novelist, and Fitz-Greene Halleck, the poet, who, speaking of the Scottish streams and their legendary associations, insisted that the American rivers were not susceptible of like [p]oetic treatment. Dana thought otherwise, and to make his [po]sition good produced three days after this poem."

It may be that Saunders wr[ote] the name Drake, for it was James Rodman Drake who [calle]d "The Culprit Fay." Perhaps it was the printer's fault tha[t the] poem is accredited to Dana. Perhaps Mr. Saunde[rs] writes so legible a hand that the printers are careless wi[th] his manuscript.

"There is," says Wheatley, [t]here is a popular notion among authors that it is not wise t[o w]rite a clear hand. Menage was one of the first to expr[ess] it. He wrote: 'If you desire that no mistake shall appea[r i]n the works which you publish, never send well-w[rit]ten copy to the printer, for in that case the manuscript is [gi]ven to young apprentices, who make a thousand errors; wh[il]e, on the other hand, that which is difficult to read is [de]alt with by the master-printers.'"

The most distressing blund[er] I ever read in print was made at the time of the burial of [the] famous antiquary and litterateur, John Payne Col[lie]r. In the London newspapers of Sept. 21, 1883, it was re[po]rted that "the remains of the late Mr. John Payne Collie[r w]ere interred yesterday in Bray churchyard, near Maidenhe[ad], in the presence of a large number of spectators." The[n ...] upon the Eastern daily press published the following re[ma]rkable perversion: "The Bray Colliery Disaster. The rem[ain]s of the late John Payne, collier, were interred yeste[rda]y afternoon in the Bray churchyard in the presence [of] a large number of friends and spectators."

Far be it from the book-lov[er] and the book-collector to rail at blunders, for not unfreq[uen]tly these very blunders make books valuable. Who cares for a Pine's Horace that does not contain the "potest" error? The genuine first edition of Hawthorne's "Scarlet Letter" is to be determined by the presence of a certain typographical slip in the introduction. The first edition of the English Scriptures printed in Ireland (1716) is much desired by collectors, and simply because of an error. Isaiah bids us "sin no more," but the Belfast printer, by some means or another, transposed the letters in such wise as to make the injunction read "sin on more."

The so-called Wicked Bible is a book that is seldom met with, and, therefore, in great demand. It was printed in the time of Charles I., and it is notorious because it omits the adverb "not" in its version of the seventh commandment; the printers were fined a large sum for this gross error. Six copies of the Wicked Bible are known to be in existence. At one time the late James Lenox had two copies; in his interesting memoirs Henry Stevens tells how he picked up one copy in Paris for fifty guineas.

Rabelais' printer got the satirical doctor into deep water for printing asne for ame; the council of the Sorbonne took the matter up and asked Francis I. to prosecute Rabelais for heresy; this the king declined to do, and Rabelais proceeded forthwith to torment the council for having founded a charge of heresy upon a printer's blunder.

Once upon a time the Foulis printing establishment at Glasgow determined to print a perfect Horace; accordingly the proof sheets were hung up at the gates of the university, and a sum of money was paid for every error detected.

Notwithstanding these precautions the edition had six uncorrected errors in it when it was finally published. Disraeli says that the so-called Pearl Bible had six thousand errata! The works of Picus Mirandula, Strasburg, 1507, gave a list of errata covering fifteen folio pages, and a worse case is that of "Missac Missalis Anatomia" (1561), a volume of one hundred and seventy-two pages, fifteen of which are devoted to the errata. The author of the Missae felt so deeply aggrieved by this array of blunders that he made a public explanation to the effect that the devil himself stole the manuscript, tampered with it, and then actually compelled the printer to misread it.

I am not sure that this ingenious explanation did not give origin to the term of "printer's devil."

It is frightful to think

What nonsense sometimes

They make of one's sense

And, what's worse, of one's rhymes.

It was only last week,

In my ode upon spring,

Which I meant to have made

A most beautiful thing,

When I talked of the dewdrops

From freshly blown roses,

The nasty things made it

From freshly blown noses.

We can fancy Richard Porson's rage (for Porson was of violent temper) when, having written the statement that "the crowd rent the air with their shouts," his printer made the line read "the crowd rent the air with their snouts." However, this error was a natural one, since it occurs in the "Catechism of the Swinish Multitude." Royalty only are privileged when it comes to the matter of blundering. When Louis XIV. was a boy he one day spoke of "un carosse"; he should have said "une carosse," but he was king, and having changed the gender of carosse the change was accepted, and unto this day carosse is masculine.

That errors should occur in newspapers is not remarkable, for much of the work in a newspaper office is done hastily. Yet some of these errors are very amusing. I remember to have read in a Berlin newspaper a number of years ago that "Prince Bismarck is trying to keep up honest and straightforward relations with all the girls" (madchen).

This statement seemed incomprehensible until it transpired that the word "madchen" was in this instance a misprint for "machten," a word meaning all the European powers.

X

WHEN FANCHON[TE?] BEWITCHED ME

The garden in which I am [   ] aying has so many diversions to catch my eye, to engage [   ] y attention and to inspire reminiscence that I find it [   ] d to treat of its beauties methodically. I find myself [   ] andering up and down, hither and thither, in so irrespons[   ] e a fashion that I marvel you have not abandoned me as [   ] e most irrational of madmen.

Yet how could it be otherw[   ]e? All around me I see those things that draw me from t[   ] pathway I set out to pursue: like a heedless butterfly I f[   ] from this sweet unto that, glorying and revelling in th[   ] sunshine and the posies. There is little that is selfish in a l[   ]e like this, and herein we have another reason why the pas[   ]on for books is beneficial. He who loves women must an[   ] hould love some one woman above the rest, and he has [   ] to his keeping, which I esteem to be one kind of se[   ]shness.

But he who truly loves boo[   ] loves all books alike, and not only this, but it grieves him [   ]at all other men do not share with him this noble passio[   ] Verily, this is the most unselfish of loves!

To return now to the matte[   ]f booksellers, I would fain impress you with the excel[   ]ces of the craft, for I know their virtues. My associatio[   ] with them has covered so long a period and has been so in[   ]nate that even in a vast multitude of people I have [   ] difficulty in determining who are the booksellers and who[   ] re not.

For, having to do with books, these men in due time come to resemble their wares not only in appearance but also in conversation. My bookseller has dwelt so long in his corner with folios and quartos and other antique tomes that he talks in black-letter and has the modest, engaging look of a brown old stout binding, and to the delectation of discriminating olfactories he exhaleth an odor of mildew and of tobacco commingled, which is more grateful to the true bibliophile than all the perfumes of Araby.

I have studied the craft so diligently that by merely clapping my eyes upon a bookseller I can tell you with certainty what manner of books he sells; but you must know that the ideal bookseller has no fads, being equally proficient in and a lover of all spheres, departments, branches, and lines of his art. He is, moreover, of a benignant nature, and he denies credit to none; yet, withal, he is righteously so discriminating that he lets the poor scholar have for a paltry sum that which the rich parvenu must pay dearly for. He is courteous and considerate where courtesy and consideration are most seemly.

Samuel Johnson once rolled into a London bookseller's shop to ask for literary employment. The bookseller scrutinized his burly frame, enormous hands, coarse face, and humble apparel.

"You would make a better porter," said he.

This was too much for the young lexicographer's patience. He picked up a folio and incontinently let fly at the bookseller's head, and then stepping over the prostrate victim he made his exit, saying: "Lie there, thou lump of lead!"

This bookseller was Osborne, who had a shop at Gray's Inn Gate. To Boswell Johnson subsequently explained: "Sir, he was impertinent to me, and I beat him."

Jacob Tonson was Dryden's bookseller; in the earlier times a seller was also a publisher of books. Dryden was not always on amiable terms with Tonson, presumably because Dryden invariably was in debt to Tonson. On one occasion Dryden asked for an advance of money, but Tonson refused upon the grounds that the poet's overdraft already exceeded the limits of reasonableness. Thereupon Dryden penned the following lines and sent them to Tonson with the message that he who wrote these lines could write more:

With leering looks, bull-faced and freckled fair

With two left legs, with Judas-colored hair,

And frowzy pores that taint the ambient air.

These lines wrought the desired effect: Tonson sent the money which Dryden had asked for. When Dryden died Tonson made overtures to Pope, but the latter soon went over to Tonson's most formidable rival, Bernard Lintot. On one occasion Pope happened to be writing to both publishers, and by a curious blunder he inclosed to each the letter intended for the other. In the letter meant for Tonson, he said that Lintot was a scoundrel, and in the letter meant for Lintot he declared that Tonson was an old rascal. We can fancy how little satisfaction Messrs. Lintot and Tonson derived from the perusal of these missent epistles.

Andrew Millar was the publisher who had practical charge of the production of Johnson's dictionary. It seems that

Johnson drew out his stipulated honorarium of eight thousand dollars (to be more exact, L1575) before the dictionary went to press; this is not surprising, for the work of preparation consumed eight years, instead of three, as Johnson had calculated. Johnson inquired of the messenger what Millar said when he received the last batch of copy. The messenger answered: "He said 'Thank God I have done with him.'" This made Johnson smile. "I am glad," said he, quietly, "that he thanks God for anything."

I was not done with my discourse when a book was brought in from Judge Methuen; the interruption was a pleasant one. "I was too busy last evening," writes the judge, "to bring you this volume which I picked up in a La Salle street stall yesterday. I know your love for the scallawag Villon, so I am sure you will fancy the lines which, evidently, the former owner of this book has scribbled upon the fly-leaf." Fancy them? Indeed I do; and if you dote on the "scallawag" as I dote on him you also will declare that our anonymous poet has not wrought ill.

FRANCOIS VILLON

If I were Francois Villon and Francois Villon I,

What would it matter to me how the time might drag or fly?

HE would in sweaty anguish toil the days and nights away,

And still not keep the prowling, growling, howling wolf at bay!

But, with my valiant bottle and my frouzy brevet-bride,

And my score of loyal cut-throats standing guard for me outside,

What worry of the morrow would provoke a casual sigh

If I were Francois Villon and Francois Villon I?

If I were Francois Villon and Francois Villon I,

To yonder gloomy boulevard at midnight I would hie;

"Stop, stranger! and deliver your possessions, ere you feel

The mettle of my bludgeon or the temper of my steel!"

He should give me gold and diamonds, his snuff-box and his cane—

"Now back, my boon companions, to our bordel with our gain!"

And, back within that brothel, how the bottles they would fly,

If I were Francois Villon and Francois Villon I!

If I were Francois Villon and Francois Villon I,

We both would mock the gibbet which the law has lifted high;

HE in his meagre, shabby home, I in my roaring den—

HE with his babes around him, I with my hunted men!

His virtue be his bulwark—my genius should be mine!—

"Go, fetch my pen, sweet Margot, and a jorum of your wine!

So would one vainly plod, and one win immortality—

If I were Francois Villon and Francois Villon I!

My acquaintance with Master Villon was made in Paris during my second visit to that fascinating capital, and for a while I was under his spell to that extent that I would read no book but his, and I made journeys to Rouen, Tours, Bordeaux, and Poitiers for the purpose of familiarizing myself with the spots where he had lived, and always under the surveillance of the police. In fact, I became so infatuated of Villonism that at one time I seriously thought of abandoning myself to a life of crime in order to emulate in certain particulars at least the example of my hero.

There were, however, hindrances to this scheme, first of which was my inability to find associates whom I wished to attach to my cause in the capacity in which Colin de Cayeulx and the Baron de Grigny served Master Francois. I sought the companionship of several low-browed, ill-favored fellows whom I believed suited to my purposes, but almost immediately I wearied of them, for they had never looked into a book and were so profoundly ignorant as to be unable to distinguish between a folio and a thirty-twomo.

Then again it befell that, while the Villon fever was raging within and I was contemplating a career of vice, I had a letter from my uncle Cephas, apprising me that Captivity Waite (she was now Mrs. Eliphalet Parker) had named her first-born after me! This intelligence had the effect of cooling and sobering me; I began to realize that, with the responsibility the coming and the christening of Captivity's first-born had imposed upon me, it behooved me to guard with exceeding jealousy the honor of the name which my namesake bore.

While I was thus tempest-tossed, Fanchonette came across my pathway, and with the appearance of Fanchonette every ambition to figure in the annals of bravado left me. Fanchonette was the niece of my landlady; her father was a perfumer; she lived with the old people in the Rue des Capucins. She was of middling stature and had blue eyes and black hair. Had she not been French, she would have been Irish, or, perhaps, a Grecian. Her manner had an indefinable charm.

It was she who acquainted me with Beranger; that is why I never take up that precious volume that I do not think, sweetly and tenderly, of Fanchonette. The book is bound, as you see, in a dainty blue, and the border toolings are delicate tracings of white—all for a purpose, I can assure you. She used to wear a dainty blue gown, from behind the nether hem of which the most immaculate of petticoats peeped out.

If we were never boys, how barren and lonely our age would be. Next to the ineffably blessed period of youth there is no time of life pleasanter than that in which serene old age reviews the exploits and the prodigies of boyhood. Ah, my gay fellows, harvest your crops diligently, that your barns and granaries be full when your arms are no longer able to wield the sickle!

Haec meminisse—to recall the old time—to see her rise out of the dear past—to hear Fanchonette's voice again—to feel the grace of springtime—how gloriously sweet this is! The little quarrels, the reconciliations, the coquetries, the jealousies, the reproaches, the forgivenesses—all the characteristic and endearing haps of the Maytime of life—precious indeed are these retrospections to the hungry eyes of age!

She wed with the perfumer's apprentice; but that was so very long ago that I can pardon, if not forget, the indiscretion. Who knows where she is to-day? Perhaps a granny beldame in a Parisian alley; perhaps for years asleep in Pere la Chaise. Come forth, beloved Beranger, and sing me the old song to make me young and strong and brave again!

Let them be served on gold—

The wealthy and the great;

Two lovers only want

A single glass and plate!

Ring ding, ring ding,

Ring ding ding—

Old wine, young lassie,

Sing, boys, sing!

XI

DIAGNOSIS OF THE BACILLUS LIBRORUM

For a good many years I was deeply interested in British politics. I was converted to Liberalism, so-called, by an incident which I deem well worth relating. One afternoon I entered a book-shop in High Holborn, and found that the Hon. William E. Gladstone had preceded me thither. I had never seen Mr. Gladstone before. I recognized him now by his resemblance to the caricatures, and by his unlikeness to the portraits which the newspapers had printed.

As I entered the shop I heard the bookseller ask: "What books shall I send?"

To this, with a very magnificent sweep of his arms indicating every point of the compass, Gladstone made answer: "Send me THOSE!"

With these words he left the place, and I stepped forward to claim a volume which had attracted my favorable attention several days previous.

"I beg your pardon, sir," said the bookseller, politely, "but that book is sold."

"Sold?" I cried.

"Yes, sir," replied the bookseller, smiling with evident pride; "Mr. Gladstone just bought it; I haven't a book for sale—Mr. Gladstone just bought them ALL!"

The bookseller then proceeded to tell me that whenever Gladstone entered a bookshop he made a practice of buying everything in sight. That magnificent, sweeping gesture of his comprehended everything—theology, history, social science, folk-lore, medicine, travel, biography—everything that came to his net was fish!

"This is the third time Mr. Gladstone has visited me," said the bookseller, "and this is the third time he has cleaned me out."

"This man is a good man," says I to myself. "So notable a lover of books surely cannot err. The cause of home rule must be a just one after all."

From others intimately acquainted with him I learned that Gladstone was an omnivorous reader; that he ordered his books by the cart-load, and that his home in Hawarden literally overflowed with books. He made a practice, I was told, of overhauling his library once in so often and of weeding out such volumes as he did not care to keep. These discarded books were sent to the second-hand dealers, and it is said that the dealers not unfrequently took advantage of Gladstone by reselling him over and over again (and at advanced prices, too) the very lots of books he had culled out and rejected.

Every book-lover has his own way of buying; so there are as many ways of buying as there are purchasers. However, Judge Methuen and I have agreed that all buyers may be classed in these following specified grand divisions:

The reckless buyer.

The shrewd buyer.

The timid buyer.

Of these three classes the third is least worthy of our consideration, although it includes very many lovers of books, and consequently very many friends of mine. I have actually known men to hesitate, to ponder, to dodder for weeks, nay, months over the purchase of a book; not because they did not want it, nor because they deemed the price exorbitant, nor yet because they were not abundantly able to pay that price. Their hesitancy was due to an innate, congenital lack of determination—that same hideous curse of vacillation which is responsible for so much misery in human life.

I have made a study of these people, and I find that most of them are bachelors whose state of singleness is due to the fact that the same hesitancy which has deprived them of many a coveted volume has operated to their discomfiture in the matrimonial sphere. While they deliberated, another bolder than they came along and walked off with the prize.

One of the gamest buyers I know of was the late John A. Rice of Chicago. As a competitor at the great auction sales he was invincible; and why? Because, having determined to buy a book, he put no limit to the amount of his bid. His instructions to his agent were in these words: "I must have those books, no matter what they cost."

An English collector found in Rice's library a set of rare volumes he had been searching for for years.

"How did you happen to get them?" he asked. "You bought them at the Spencer sale and against my bid. Do you know, I told my buyer to bid a thousand pounds for them, if necessary!"

"That was where I had the advantage of you," said Rice, quietly. "I specified no limit; I simply told my man to buy the books."

The spirit of the collector cropped out early in Rice. I remember to have heard him tell how one time, when he was a young man, he was shuffling over a lot of tracts in a bin in front of a Boston bookstall. His eye suddenly fell upon a little pamphlet entitled "The Cow-Chace." He picked it up and read it. It was a poem founded upon the defeat of Generals Wayne, Irving, and Proctor. The last stanza ran in this wise:

And now I've closed my epic strain,

I tremble as I show it,

Lest this same warrior-drover, Wayne,

Should ever catch the poet.

Rice noticed that the pamphlet bore the imprint of James Rivington, New York, 1780. It occurred to him that some time this modest tract of eighteen pages might be valuable; at any rate, he paid the fifteen cents demanded for it, and at the same time he purchased for ten cents another pamphlet entitled "The American Tories, a Satire."

Twenty years later, having learned the value of these exceedingly rare tracts, Mr. Rice sent them to London and had them bound in Francis Bedford's best style—"crimson crushed levant morocco, finished to a Grolier pattern." Bedford's charges amounted to seventy-five dollars, which with the original cost of the pamphlets represented an expenditure of seventy-five dollars and twenty-five cents upon Mr. Rice's part. At the sale of the Rice library in 1870, however, this curious, rare, and beautiful little book brought the extraordinary sum of seven hundred and fifty dollars!

The Rice library contained about five thousand volumes, and it realized at auction sale somewhat more than seventy-two thousand dollars. Rice has often told me that for a long time he could not make up his mind to part with his books; yet his health was so poor that he found it imperative to retire from business, and to devote a long period of time to travel; these were the considerations that induced him finally to part with his treasures. "I have never regretted having sold them," he said. "Two years after the sale the Chicago fire came along. Had I retained those books, every one of them would have been lost."

Mrs. Rice shared her husband's enthusiasm for books. Whenever a new invoice arrived, the two would lock themselves in their room, get down upon their knees on the floor, open the box, take out the treasures and gloat over them, together! Noble lady! she was such a wife as any good man might be proud of. They were very happy in their companionship on earth, were my dear old friends. He was the first to go; their separation was short; together once more and forever they share the illimitable joys which await all lovers of good books when virtue hath mournfully writ the colophon to their human careers.

Although Mr. Rice survived the sale of his remarkable library a period of twenty-six years, he did not get together again a collection of books that he was willing to call a library. His first collection was so remarkable that he preferred to have his fame rest wholly upon it. Perhaps he was wise; yet how few collectors there are who would have done as he did.

As for myself, I verily believe that, if by fire or by water my library should be destroyed this night, I should start in again to-morrow upon the collection of another library. Or if I did not do this, I should lay myself down to die, for how could I live without the companionships to which I have ever been accustomed, and which have grown as dear to me as life itself?

Whenever Judge Methuen is in a jocular mood and wishes to tease me, he asks me whether I have forgotten the time when I was possessed of a spirit of reform and registered a solemn vow in high heaven to buy no more books. Teasing, says Victor Hugo, is the malice of good men; Judge Methuen means no evil when he recalls that weakness—the one weakness in all my career.

No, I have not forgotten that time; I look back upon it with a shudder of horror, for wretched indeed would have been my existence had I carried into effect the project I devised at that remote period!

Dr. O'Rell has an interesting theory which you will find recorded in the published proceedings of the National Academy of Sciences (vol. xxxiv., p. 216). Or, if you cannot procure copies of that work, it may serve your purpose to know that the doctor's theory is to this effect—viz., that bibliomania does not deserve the name of bibliomania until it is exhibited in the second stage. For secondary bibliomania there is no known cure; the few cases reported as having been cured were doubtless not bibliomania at all, or, at least, were what we of the faculty call false or chicken bibliomania.

"In false bibliomania, which," says Dr. O'Rell, "is the primary stage of the grand passion—the vestibule to the main edifice—the usual symptoms are flushed cheeks, sparkling eyes, a bounding pulse, and quick respiration. This period of exaltation is not unfrequently followed by a condition of collapse in which we find the victim pale, pulseless, and dejected. He is pursued and tormented of imaginary horrors, he reproaches himself for imaginary crimes, and he implores piteously for relief from fancied dangers. The sufferer now stands in a slippery place; unless his case is treated intelligently he will issue from that period of gloom cured of the sweetest of madnesses, and doomed to a life of singular uselessness.

"But properly treated," continues Dr. O'Rell, "and particularly if his spiritual needs be ministered to, he can be brought safely through this period of collapse into a condition of reenforced exaltation, which is the true, or secondary stage of, bibliomania, and for which there is no cure known to humanity."

I should trust Dr. O'Rell's judgment in this matter, even if I did not know from experience that it was true. For Dr. O'Rell is the most famous authority we have in bibliomania and kindred maladies. It is he (I make the information known at the risk of offending the ethics of the profession)—it is he who discovered the bacillus librorum, and, what is still more important and still more to his glory, it is he who invented that subtle lymph which is now everywhere employed by the profession as a diagnostic where the presence of the germs of bibliomania (in other words, bacilli librorum) is suspected.

I once got this learned scientist to inject a milligram of the lymph into the femoral artery of Miss Susan's cat. Within an hour the precocious beast surreptitiously entered my library for the first time in her life, and ate the covers of my pet edition of Rabelais. This demonstrated to Dr. O'Rell's satisfaction the efficacy of his diagnostic, and it proved to Judge Methuen's satisfaction what the Judge has always maintained—viz., that Rabelais was an old rat.

XII

THE PLEASURES OF EXTRA-ILLUSTRATION

Very many years ago we became convinced—Judge Methuen and I did—that there was nothing new in the world. I think it was while we were in London and while we were deep in the many fads of bibliomania that we arrived at this important conclusion.

We had been pursuing with enthusiasm the exciting delights of extra-illustration, a practice sometimes known as Grangerism; the friends of the practice call it by the former name, the enemies by the latter. We were engaged at extra-illustrating Boswell's life of Johnson, and had already got together somewhat more than eleven thousand prints when we ran against a snag, an obstacle we never could surmount. We agreed that our work would be incomplete, and therefore vain, unless we secured a picture of the book with which the great lexicographer knocked down Osborne, the bookseller at Gray's Inn Gate.

Unhappily we were wholly in the dark as to what the title of that book was, and, although we ransacked the British Museum and even appealed to the learned Frognall Dibdin, we could not get a clew to the identity of the volume. To be wholly frank with you, I will say that both the Judge and I had wearied of the occupation; moreover, it involved great expense, since we were content with nothing but India proofs (those before letters preferred). So we were glad of this excuse for abandoning the practice.

While we were contemplating a graceful retreat the Judge happened to discover in the "Natural History" of Pliny a passage which proved to our satisfaction that, so far from being a new or a modern thing, the extra-illustration of books was of exceptional antiquity. It seems that Atticus, the friend of Cicero, wrote a book on the subject of portraits and portrait-painting, in the course of which treatise he mentions that Marcus Varro "conceived the very liberal idea of inserting, by some means or another, in his numerous volumes, the portraits of several hundred individuals, as he could not bear the idea that all traces of their features should be lost or that the lapse of centuries should get the better of mankind."

"Thus," says Pliny, "was he the inventor of a benefit to his fellow-men that might have been envied by the gods themselves; for not only did he confer immortality upon the originals of these portraits, but he transmitted these portraits to all parts of the earth, so that everywhere it might be possible for them to be present, and for each to occupy his niche."

Now, Pliny is not the only one who has contributed to the immortalization of Marcus Varro. I have had among my papers for thirty years the verses which Judge Methuen dashed off (for poets invariably dash off their poetry), and they are such pleasant verses that I don't mind letting the world see them.

MARCUS VARRO

Marcus Varro went up and down

The places where old books were sold;

He ransacked all the shops in town

For pictures new and pictures old.

He gave the folk of earth no peace;

Snooping around by day and night,

He plied the trade in Rome and Greece

Of an insatiate Grangerite.

"Pictures!" was evermore his cry—

"Pictures of old or recent date,"

And pictures only would he buy

Wherewith to "extra-illustrate."

Full many a tome of ancient type

And many a manuscript he took,

For nary purpose but to swipe

Their pictures for some other book.

While Marcus Varro plied his fad

There was not in the shops of Greece

A book or pamphlet to be had

That was not minus frontispiece.

Nor did he hesitate to ply

His baleful practices at home;

It was not possible to buy

A perfect book in all of Rome!

What must the other folk have done—

Who, glancing o'er the books they bought,

Came soon and suddenly upon

The vandalism Varro wrought!

How must their cheeks have flamed with red—

How did their hearts with choler beat!

We can imagine what they said—

We can imagine, not repeat!

Where are the books that Varro made—

The pride of dilettante Rome—

With divers portraitures inlaid

Swiped from so many another tome?

The worms devoured them long ago—

O wretched worms! ye should have fed

Not on the books "extended" so,

But on old Varro's flesh instead!

Alas, that Marcus Varro lives

And is a potent factor yet!

Alas, that still his practice gives

Good men occasion for regret!

To yonder bookstall, pri'thee, go,

And by the "missing" prints and plates

And frontispieces you shall know

He lives, and "extra-illustrates"!

In justice to the Judge and to myself I should say that neither of us wholly approves the sentiment which the poem I have quoted implies. We regard Grangerism as one of the unfortunate stages in bibliomania; it is a period which seldom covers more than five years, although Dr. O'Rell has met with one case in his practice that has lasted ten years and still gives no symptom of abating in virulence.

Humanity invariably condones the pranks of youth on the broad and charitable grounds that "boys will be boys"; so we bibliomaniacs are prone to wink at the follies of the Grangerite, for we know that he will know better by and by and will heartily repent of the mischief he has done. We know the power of books so well that we know that no man can have to do with books that presently he does not love them. He may at first endure them; then he may come only to pity them; anon, as surely as the morrow's sun riseth, he shall embrace and love those precious things.

So we say that we would put no curb upon any man, it being better that many books should be destroyed, if ultimately by that destruction a penitent and loyal soul be added to the roster of bibliomaniacs. There is more joy over one Grangerite that repenteth than over ninety and nine just men that need no repentance.

And we have a similar feeling toward such of our number as for the nonce become imbued with a passion for any of the other little fads which bibliomaniac flesh is heir to. All the soldiers in an army cannot be foot, or horse, or captains, or majors, or generals, or artillery, or ensigns, or drummers, or buglers. Each one has his place to fill and his part to do, and the consequence is a concinnate whole. Bibliomania is beautiful as an entirety, as a symmetrical blending of a multitude of component parts, and he is indeed disloyal to the cause who, through envy or shortsightedness or ignorance, argues to the discredit of angling, or Napoleonana, or balladry, or Indians, or Burns, or Americana, or any other branch or phase of bibliomania; for each of these things accomplishes a noble purpose in that each contributes to the glory of the great common cause of bibliomania, which is indeed the summum bonum of human life.

I have heard many decried who indulged their fancy for bookplates, as if, forsooth, if a man loved his books, he should not lavish upon them testimonials of his affection! Who that loves his wife should hesitate to buy adornments for her person? I favor everything that tends to prove that the human heart is swayed by the tenderer emotions. Gratitude is surely one of the noblest emotions of which humanity is capable, and he is indeed unworthy of our respect who would forbid humanity's expressing in every dignified and reverential manner its gratitude for the benefits conferred by the companionship of books.

As for myself, I urge upon all lovers of books to provide themselves with bookplates. Whenever I see a book that bears its owner's plate I feel myself obligated to treat that book with special consideration. It carries with it a certificate of its master's love; the bookplate gives the volume a certain status it would not otherwise have. Time and again I have fished musty books out of bins in front of bookstalls, bought them and borne them home with me simply because they had upon their covers the bookplates of their former owners. I have a case filled with these aristocratic estrays, and I insist that they shall be as carefully dusted and kept as my other books, and I have provided in my will for their perpetual maintenance after my decease.

If I were a rich man I should found a hospital for homeless aristocratic books, an institution similar in all essential particulars to the institution which is now operated at our national capital under the bequest of the late Mr. Cochrane. I should name it the Home for Genteel Volumes in Decayed Circumstances.

I was a young man when I adopted the bookplate which I am still using, and which will be found in all my books. I drew the design myself and had it executed by a son of Anderson, the first of American engravers. It is by no means elaborate: a book rests upon a heart, and underneath appear the lines:

My Book and Heart

Must never part.

Ah, little Puritan maid, with thy dear eyes of honest blue and thy fair hair in proper plaits adown thy back, little thought we that springtime long ago back among the New England hills that the tiny book we read together should follow me through all my life! What a part has that Primer played! And now all these other beloved companions bear witness to the love I bear that Primer and its teachings, for each wears the emblem I plucked from its homely pages.

That was in the springtime, Captivity Waite; anon came summer, with all its exuberant glory, and presently the cheery autumn stole upon me. And now it is the wintertime, and under the snows lies buried many a sweet, fair thing I cherished once. I am aweary and will rest a little while; lie thou there, my pen, for a dream—a pleasant dream—calleth me away. I shall see those distant hills again, and the homestead under the elms; the old associations and the old influences shall be round about me, and a child shall lead me and we shall go together through green pastures and by still waters. And, O my pen, it will be the springtime again!

XIII

ON THE ODORS WHICH MY BOOKS EXHALE

Have you ever come out of the thick, smoky atmosphere of the town into the fragrant, gracious atmosphere of a library? If you have, you know how grateful the change is, and you will agree with me when I say that nothing else is so quieting to the nerves, so conducive to physical health, and so quick to restore a lively flow of the spirits.

Lafcadio Hearn once wrote a treatise upon perfumes, an ingenious and scholarly performance; he limited the edition to fifty copies and published it privately—so the book is rarely met with. Curiously enough, however, this author had nothing to say in the book about the smells of books, which I regard as a most unpardonable error, unless, properly estimating the subject to be worthy of a separate treatise, he has postponed its consideration and treatment to a time when he can devote the requisite study and care to it.

We have it upon the authority of William Blades that books breathe; however, the testimony of experts is not needed upon this point, for if anybody be sceptical, all he has to do to convince himself is to open a door of a bookcase at any time and his olfactories will be greeted by an outrush of odors that will prove to him beyond all doubt that books do actually consume air and exhale perfumes.

Visitors to the British Museum complain not unfrequently that they are overcome by the closeness of the atmosphere in that place, and what is known as the British Museum headache has come to be recognized by the medical profession in London as a specific ailment due to the absence of oxygen in the atmosphere, which condition is caused by the multitude of books, each one of which, by that breathing process peculiar to books, consumes several thousand cubic feet of air every twenty-four hours.

Professor Huxley wondered for a long time why the atmosphere of the British Museum should be poisonous while other libraries were free from the poison; a series of experiments convinced him that the presence of poison in the atmosphere was due to the number of profane books in the Museum. He recommended that these poison-engendering volumes be treated once every six months with a bath of cedria, which, as I understand, is a solution of the juices of the cedar tree; this, he said, would purge the mischievous volumes temporarily of their evil propensities and abilities.

I do not know whether this remedy is effective, but I remember to have read in Pliny that cedria was used by the ancients to render their manuscripts imperishable. When Cneius Terentius went digging in his estate in the Janiculum he came upon a coffer which contained not only the remains of Numa, the old Roman king, but also the manuscripts of the famous laws which Numa compiled. The king was in some such condition as you might suppose him to be after having been buried several centuries, but the manuscripts were as fresh as new, and their being so is said to have been due to the fact that before their burial they were rubbed with citrus leaves.

These so-called books of Numa would perhaps have been preserved unto this day but for the fanaticism of the people who exhumed and read them; they were promptly burned by Quintus Petilius, the praetor, because (as Cassius

Hemina explains) they treated of philosophical subjects, or because, as Livy testifies, their doctrines were inimical to the religion then existing.

As I have had little to do with profane literature, I know nothing of the habits of such books as Professor Huxley has prescribed an antidote against. Of such books as I have gathered about me and made my constant companions I can say truthfully that a more delectable-flavored lot it were impossible to find. As I walk amongst them, touching first this one and then that, and regarding all with glances of affectionate approval, I fancy that I am walking in a splendid garden, full of charming vistas, wherein parterre after parterre of beautiful flowers is unfolded to my enraptured vision; and surely there never were other odors so delightful as the odors which my books exhale!

My garden aboundeth in pleasant nooks

And fragrance is over it all;

For sweet is the smell of my old, old books

In their places against the wall.

Here is a folio that's grim with age

And yellow and green with mould;

There's the breath of the sea on every page

And the hint of a stanch ship's hold.

And here is a treasure from France la belle

Exhaleth a faint perfume

Of wedded lily and asphodel

In a garden of song abloom.

And this wee little book of Puritan mien

And rude, conspicuous print

Hath the Yankee flavor of wintergreen,

Or, may be, of peppermint.

In Walton the brooks a-babbling tell

Where the cheery daisy grows,

And where in meadow or woodland dwell

The buttercup and the rose.

But best beloved of books, I ween,

Are those which one perceives

Are hallowed by ashes dropped between

The yellow, well-thumbed leaves.

For it's here a laugh and it's there a tear,
Till the treasured book is read;
And the ashes betwixt the pages here
Tell us of one long dead.

But the gracious presence reappears
As we read the book again,
And the fragrance of precious, distant years
Filleth the hearts of men

Come, pluck with me in my garden nooks
The posies that bloom for all;
Oh, sweet is the smell of my old, old books
In their places against the wall!

Better than flowers are they, these books of mine! For what are the seasons to them? Neither can the drought of summer nor the asperity of winter wither or change them. At all times and under all circumstances they are the same—radiant, fragrant, hopeful, helpful! There is no charm which they do not possess, no beauty that is not theirs.

What wonder is it that from time immemorial humanity has craved the boon of carrying to the grave some book particularly beloved in life? Even Numa Pompilius provided that his books should share his tomb with him. Twenty-four of these precious volumes were consigned with him to the grave. When Gabriel Rossetti's wife died, the poet cast into her open grave the unfinished volume of his poems, that being the last and most precious tribute he could pay to her cherished memory.

History records instance after instance of the consolation dying men have received from the perusal of books, and many a one has made his end holding in his hands a particularly beloved volume. The reverence which even unlearned men have for books appeals in these splendid libraries which are erected now and again with funds provided by the wills of the illiterate. How dreadful must be the last moments of that person who has steadfastly refused to share the companionship and acknowledge the saving grace of books!

Such, indeed, is my regard for these friendships that it is with misery that I contemplate the probability of separation from them by and by. I have given my friends to understand that when I am done with earth certain of my books shall be buried with me. The list of these books will be found in the left-hand upper drawer of the old mahogany secretary in the front spare room.

When I am done,

I'd have no son

Pounce on these treasures like a vulture;

Nay, give them half

My epitaph

And let them share in my sepulture.

Then when the crack

Of doom rolls back

The marble and the earth that hide me,

I'll smuggle home

Each precious tome

Without a fear a wife shall chide me.

The dread of being separated by death from the objects of one's love has pursued humanity from the beginning. The Hindoos used to have a selfish fashion of requiring their widows to be entombed alive with their corpses. The North American Indian insists that his horse, his bow and arrows, his spear, and his other cherished trinkets shall share his grave with him.

My sister, Miss Susan, has provided that after her demise a number of her most prized curios shall be buried with her. The list, as I recall it, includes a mahogany four-post bedstead, an Empire dresser, a brass warming-pan, a pair of brass andirons, a Louis Quinze table, a Mayflower teapot, a Tomb of Washington platter, a pewter tankard, a pair of her grandmother's candlesticks, a Paul Revere lantern, a tall Dutch clock, a complete suit of armor purchased in Rome, and a collection of Japanese bric-a-brac presented to Miss Susan by a returned missionary.

I do not see what Miss Susan can possibly do with all this trumpery in the hereafter, but, if I survive her, I shall certainly insist upon a compliance with her wishes, even though it involve the erection of a tumulus as prodigious as the pyramid of Cheops.

XIV

ELZEVIRS AND DIVERS OTHER MATTERS

Boswell's "Life of Johnson" and Lockhart's "Life of Scott" are accepted as the models of biography. The third remarkable performance in this line is Mrs. Gordon's memoir of her father, John Wilson, a volume so charmingly and tenderly written as to be of interest to those even who know and care little about that era in the history of English literature in which "crusty Christopher" and his associates in the making of "Blackwood's" figured.

It is a significant fact, I think, that the three greatest biographers the world has known should have been Scotch; it has long been the fashion to laugh and to sneer at what is called Scotch dulness; yet what prodigies has not Scotch genius performed in every department of literature, and would not our literature be poor indeed to-day but for the contributions which have been made to it by the very people whom we affect to deride?

John Wilson was one of the most interesting figures of a time when learning was at a premium; he was a big man amongst big men, and even in this irreverential time genius uncovers at the mention of his name. His versatility was astounding; with equal facility and felicity he could conduct a literary symposium and a cock-fight, a theological discussion and an angling expedition, a historical or a political inquiry and a fisticuffs.

Nature had provided him with a mighty brain in a powerful body; he had a physique equal to the performance of what suggestion soever his splendid intellectuals made. To him the incredible feat of walking seventy miles within the compass of a day was mere child's play; then, when the printer became clamorous, he would immure himself in his wonderful den and reel off copy until that printer cried "Hold; enough!" It was no unusual thing for him to write for thirteen hours at a stretch; when he worked he worked, and when he played he played—that is perhaps the reason why he was never a dull boy.

Wilson seems to have been a procrastinator. He would put off his task to the very last moment; this is a practice that is common with literary men—in fact, it was encouraged by those who were regarded as authorities in such matters anciently. Ringelbergius gave this advice to an author under his tuition:

"Tell the printers," said he, "to make preparations for a work you intend writing, and never alarm yourself about it because it is not even begun, for, after having announced it you may without difficulty trace out in your own head the whole plan of your work and its divisions, after which compose the arguments of the chapters, and I can assure you that in this manner you may furnish the printers daily with more copy than they want. But, remember, when you have once begun there must be no flagging till the work is finished."

The loyalty of human admiration was never better illustrated than in Shelton Mackenzie's devotion to Wilson's genius. To Mackenzie we are indebted for a compilation of the "Noctes Ambrosianae," edited with such discrimination, such ability, such learning, and such enthusiasm that, it seems to me, the work must endure as a monument not only to Wilson's but also to Mackenzie's genius.

I have noticed one peculiarity that distinguishes many admirers of the Noctes: they seldom care to read anything else; in the Noctes they find a response to the demand of every mood. It is much the same way with lovers of Father Prout. Dr. O'Rell divides his adoration between old Kit North and the sage of Watergrass Hill. To be bitten of either mania is bad enough; when one is possessed at the same time of a passion both for the Noctes and for the Reliques hopeless indeed is his malady! Dr. O'Rell is so deep under the spell of crusty Christopher and the Corkonian pere that he not only buys every copy of the Noctes and of the Reliques he comes across, but insists upon giving copies of these books to everybody in his acquaintance. I have even known him to prescribe one or the other of these works to patients of his.

I recall that upon one occasion, having lost an Elzevir at a book auction, I was afflicted with melancholia to such a degree that I had to take to my bed. Upon my physician's arrival he made, as is his custom, a careful inquiry into my condition and into the causes inducing it. Finally, "You are afflicted," said Dr. O'Rell, "with the megrims, which, fortunately, is at present confined to the region of the Pacchionian depressions of the sinister parietal. I shall administer Father Prout's 'Rogueries of Tom Moore' (pronounced More) and Kit North's debate with the Ettrick Shepherd upon the subject of sawmon. No other remedy will prove effective."

The treatment did, in fact, avail me, for within forty-eight hours I was out of bed, and out of the house; and, what is better yet, I picked up at a bookstall, for a mere song, a first edition of "Special Providences in New England"!

Never, however, have I wholly ceased to regret the loss of the Elzevir, for an Elzevir is to me one of the most gladdening sights human eye can rest upon. In his life of the elder Aldus, Renouard says: "How few are there of those who esteem and pay so dearly for these pretty editions who know that the type that so much please them are the work of Francis Garamond, who cast them one hundred years before at Paris."

In his bibliographical notes (a volume seldom met with now) the learned William Davis records that Louis Elzevir was the first who observed the distinction between the v consonant and the u vowel, which distinction, however, had been recommended long before by Ramus and other writers, but had never been regarded. There were five of these Elzevirs, viz.: Louis, Bonaventure, Abraham, Louis, Jr., and Daniel.

A hundred years ago a famous bibliophile remarked: "The diminutiveness of a large portion, and the beauty of the whole, of the classics printed by the Elzevirs at Leyden and Amsterdam have long rendered them justly celebrated, and the prices they bear in public sales sufficiently demonstrate the estimation in which they are at present held."

The regard for these precious books still obtains, and we meet with it in curiously out-of-the-way places, as well as in those libraries where one would naturally expect to find it. My young friend Irving Way (himself a collector of rare enthusiasm) tells me that recently during a pilgrimage through the state of Texas he came upon a gentleman who showed him in his modest home the most superb collection of Elzevirs he had ever set eyes upon!

How far-reaching is thy grace, O bibliomania! How good and sweet it is that no distance, no environment, no poverty, no distress can appall or stay thee. Like that grim spectre we call death, thou knockest impartially at the palace portal and at the cottage door. And it seemeth thy especial delight to bring unto the lonely in desert places the companionship that exalteth humanity!

It makes me groan to think of the number of Elzevirs that are lost in the libraries of rich parvenus who know nothing of and care no thing for the treasures about them further than a certain vulgar vanity which is involved. When Catherine of Russia wearied of Koritz she took to her affection one Kimsky Kossakof, a sergeant in the guards. Kimsky was elated by this sudden acquisition of favor and riches. One of his first orders was to his bookseller. Said he to that worthy: "Fit me up a handsome library; little books above and great ones below."

It is narrated of a certain British warrior that upon his retirement from service he bought a library en bloc, and, not knowing any more about books than a peccary knows of the harmonies of the heavenly choir, he gave orders for the arrangement of the volumes in this wise: "Range me," he quoth, "the grenadiers (folios) at the bottom, the battalion (octavos) in the middle, and the light-bobs (duodecimos) at the top!"

Samuel Johnson, dancing attendance upon Lord Chesterfield, could hardly have felt his humiliation more keenly than did the historian Gibbon when his grace the Duke of Cumberland met him bringing the third volume of his "Decline and Fall of the Roman Empire" to the ducal mansion. This history was originally printed in quarto; Gibbon was carrying the volume and anticipating the joy of the duke upon its arrival. What did the duke say? "What?" he cried. "Ah, another —— big square book, eh?"

It is the fashion nowadays to harp upon the degeneracy of humanity; to insist that taste is corrupted, and that the faculty of appreciation is dead. We seem incapable of realizing that this is the golden age of authors, if not the golden age of authorship.

In the good old days authors were in fact a despised and neglected class. The Greeks put them to death, as the humor seized them. For a hundred years after his death Shakespeare was practically unknown to his countrymen, except Suckling and his coterie: during his life he was roundly assailed by his contemporaries, one of the latter going to the extreme of denouncing him as a daw that strutted in borrowed plumage. Milton was accused of plagiarism, and one of his critics devoted many years to compiling from every quarter passages in ancient works which bore a similarity to the blind poet's verses. Even Samuel Johnson's satire of "London" was pronounced a plagiarism.

The good old days were the days, seemingly, when the critics had their way and ran things with a high hand; they made or unmade books and authors. They killed Chatterton, just as, some years later, they hastened the death of Keats. For a time they were all-powerful. It was not until the end of the eighteenth century that these professional tyrants began to lose their grip, and when Byron took up the lance against them their doom was practically sealed.

Who would care a picayune in these degenerate days what Dr. Warburton said pro or con a book? It was Warburton (then Bishop of Gloucester) who remarked of Granger's "Biographical History of England" that it was "an odd one." This was as high a compliment as he ever paid a book; those which he did not like he called sad books, and those which he fancied he called odd ones.

The truth seems to be that through the diffusion of knowledge and the multiplicity and cheapness of books people generally have reached the point in intelligence where they feel warranted in asserting their ability to judge for themselves. So the occupation of the critic, as interpreted and practised of old, is gone.

Reverting to the practice of lamenting the degeneracy of humanity, I should say that the fashion is by no means a new one. Search the records of the ancients and you will find the same harping upon the one string of present decay and former virtue. Herodotus, Sallust, Caesar, Cicero, and Pliny take up and repeat the lugubrious tale in turn.

Upon earth there are three distinct classes of men: Those who contemplate the past, those who contemplate the present, those who contemplate the future. I am of those who believe that humanity progresses, and it is my theory that the best works of the past have survived and come down to us in these books which are our dearest legacies, our proudest possessions, and our best-beloved companions.

XV

A BOOK THAT BRINGS SOLACE AND CHEER

One of my friends had a mania for Bunyan once upon a time, and, although he has now abandoned that fad for the more fashionable passion of Napoleonana, he still exhibits with evident pride the many editions of the "Pilgrim's Progress" he gathered together years ago. I have frequently besought him to give me one of his copies, which has a curious frontispiece illustrating the dangers besetting the traveller from the City of Destruction to the Celestial City. This frontispiece, which is prettily illuminated, occurs in Virtue's edition of the "Pilgrim's Progress"; the book itself is not rare, but it is hardly procurable in perfect condition, for the reason that the colored plate is so pleasing to the eye that few have been able to resist the temptation to make away with it.

For similar reasons it is seldom that we meet with a perfect edition of Quarles' "Emblems"; indeed, an "Emblems" of early publication that does not lack the title-page is a great rarity. In the "good old days," when juvenile books were few, the works of Bunyan and of Quarles were vastly popular with the little folk, and little fingers wrought sad havoc with the title-pages and the pictures that with their extravagant and vivid suggestions appealed so directly and powerfully to the youthful fancy.

Coleridge says of the "Pilgrim's Progress" that it is the best summary of evangelical Christianity ever produced by a writer not miraculously inspired. Froude declares that it has for two centuries affected the spiritual opinions of the

English race in every part of the world more powerfully than any other book, except the Bible. "It is," says Macaulay, "perhaps the only book about which, after the lapse of a hundred years, the educated minority has come over to the opinion of the common people."

Whether or not Bunyan is, as D'Israeli has called him, the Spenser of the people, and whether or not his work is the poetry of Puritanism, the best evidence of the merit of the "Pilgrim's Progress" appears, as Dr. Johnson has shrewdly pointed out, in the general and continued approbation of mankind. Southey has critically observed that to his natural style Bunyan is in some degree beholden for his general popularity, his language being everywhere level to the most ignorant reader and to the meanest capacity; "there is a homely reality about it—a nursery tale is not more intelligible, in its manner of narration, to a child."

Another cause of his popularity, says Southey, is that he taxes the imagination as little as the understanding. "The vividness of his own, which, as history shows, sometimes could not distinguish ideal impressions from actual ones, occasioned this. He saw the things of which he was writing as distinctly with his mind's eye as if they were, indeed, passing before him in a dream."

It is clear to me that in his youth Bunyan would have endeared himself to me had I lived at that time, for his fancy was of that kind and of such intensity as I delight to find in youth. "My sins," he tells us, "did so offend the Lord that even in my childhood He did scare and affright me with fearful dreams and did terrify me with dreadful visions. I have been in my bed greatly afflicted, while asleep, with apprehensions of devils and wicked spirits, who still, as I then thought, labored to draw me away with them, of which I could never be rid."

It is quite likely that Bunyan overestimated his viciousness. One of his ardent, intense temperament having once been touched of the saving grace could hardly help recognizing in himself the most miserable of sinners. It is related that upon one occasion he was going somewhere disguised as a wagoner, when he was overtaken by a constable who had a warrant for his arrest.

"Do you know that devil of a fellow Bunyan?" asked the constable.

"Know him?" cried Bunyan. "You might call him a devil indeed, if you knew him as well as I once did!"

This was not the only time his wit served him to good purpose. On another occasion a certain Cambridge student, who was filled with a sense of his own importance, undertook to prove to him what a divine thing reason was, and he capped his argument with the declaration that reason was the chief glory of man which distinguished him from a beast. To this Bunyan calmly made answer: "Sin distinguishes man from beast; is sin divine?"

Frederick Saunders observes that, like Milton in his blindness, Bunyan in his imprisonment had his spiritual perception made all the brighter by his exclusion from the glare of the outside world. And of the great debt of gratitude we all owe to "the wicked tinker of Elstow" Dean Stanley has spoken so truly that I am fain to quote his words: "We all need to be cheered by the help of Greatheart and Standfast and Valiant-for-the-Truth, and good old Honesty! Some of us have been in Doubting

Castle, some in the Slough of Despond. Some have experienced the temptations of Vanity Fair; all of us have to climb the Hill of Difficulty; all of us need to be instructed by the Interpreter in the House Beautiful; all of us bear the same burden; all of us need the same armor in our fight with Apollyon; all of us have to pass through the Wicket Gate—to pass through the dark river, and for all of us (if God so will) there wait the shining ones at the gates of the Celestial City! Who does not love to linger over the life story of the 'immortal dreamer' as one of those characters for whom man has done so little and God so much?"

About my favorite copy of the "Pilgrim's Progress" many a pleasant reminiscence lingers, for it was one of the books my grandmother gave my father when he left home to engage in the great battle of life; when my father died this thick, dumpy little volume, with its rude cuts and poorly printed pages, came into my possession. I do not know what part this book played in my father's life, but I can say for myself that it has brought me solace and cheer a many times.

The only occasion upon which I felt bitterly toward Dr. O'Rell was when that personage observed in my hearing one day that Bunyan was a dyspeptic, and that had he not been one he would doubtless never have written the "Pilgrim's Progress."

I took issue with the doctor on this point; whereupon he cited those visions and dreams, which, according to the light of science as it now shines, demonstrate that Bunyan's digestion must have been morbid. And, forthwith, he overwhelmed me with learned instances from Galen and Hippocrates, from Spurzheim and Binns, from Locke and

Beattie, from Malebranche and Bertholini, from Darwin and Descartes, from Charlevoix and Berkeley, from Heraclitus and Blumenbach, from Priestley and Abercrombie; in fact, forsooth, he quoted me so many authorities that it verily seemed to me as though the whole world were against me!

I did not know until then that Dr. O'Rell had made a special study of dreams, of their causes and of their signification. I had always supposed that astrology was his particular hobby, in which science I will concede him to be deeply learned, even though he has never yet proved to my entire satisfaction that the reason why my copy of Justinian has faded from a royal purple to a pale blue is, first, because the binding was renewed at the wane of the moon and when Sirius was in the ascendant, and, secondly, because (as Dr. O'Rell has discovered) my binder was born at a moment fifty-six years ago when Mercury was in the fourth house and Herschel and Saturn were aspected in conjunction, with Sol at his northern declination.

Dr. O'Rell has frequently expressed surprise that I have never wearied of and drifted away from the book-friendships of my earlier years. Other people, he says, find, as time elapses, that they no longer discover those charms in certain books which attracted them so powerfully in youth. "We have in our earlier days," argues the doctor, "friendships so dear to us that we would repel with horror the suggestion that we could ever become heedless or forgetful of them; yet, alas, as we grow older we gradually become indifferent to these first friends, and we are weaned from them by other friendships; there even comes a time when we actually wonder how it were possible for us to be on terms of intimacy with such or such a person. We grow away from people, and in like manner and for similar reasons we grow away from books."

Is it indeed possible for one to become indifferent to an object he has once loved? I can hardly believe so. At least it is not so with me, and, even though the time may come when I shall no longer be able to enjoy the uses of these dear old friends with the old-time enthusiasm, I should still regard them with that tender reverence which in his age the poet Longfellow expressed when looking round upon his beloved books:

Sadly as some old mediaeval knight

Gazed at the arms he could no longer wield—

The sword two-handed and the shining shield

Suspended in the hall and full in sight,

While secret longings for the lost delight

Of tourney or adventure in the field

Came over him, and tears but half concealed

Trembled and fell upon his beard of white;

So I behold these books upon their shelf

My ornaments and arms of other days;

Not wholly useless, though no longer used,

For they remind me of my other self

Younger and stronger, and the pleasant ways

In which I walked, now clouded and confused.

If my friend O'Rell's theory be true, how barren would be Age! Lord Bacon tells us in his "Apothegms" that Alonzo of Aragon was wont to say, in commendation of Age, that Age appeared to be best in four things: Old wood best to burn; old wine to drink; old friends to trust; and old authors to read. Sir John Davys recalls that "a French writer (whom I love well) speaks of three kinds of companions: Men, women and books," and my revered and beloved poet-friend, Richard Henry Stoddard, has wrought out this sentiment in a poem of exceeding beauty, of which the concluding stanza runs in this wise:

Better than men and women, friend,

That are dust, though dear in our joy and pain,

Are the books their cunning hands have penned,

For they depart, but the books remain;

Through these they speak to us what was best

In the loving heart and the noble mind;

All their royal souls possessed

Belongs forever to all mankind!

When others fail him, the wise man looks

To the sure companionship of books.

If ever, O honest friends of mine, I should forget you or weary of your companionship, whither would depart the memories and the associations with which each of you is hallowed! Would ever the modest flowers of spring-time, budding in pathways where I no longer wander, recall to my failing sight the vernal beauty of the Puritan maid, Captivity? In what reverie of summer-time should I feel again the graciousness of thy presence, Yseult?

And Fanchonette—sweet, timid little Fanchonette! would ever thy ghost come back from out those years away off yonder? Be hushed, my Beranger, for a moment; another song hath awakened softly responsive echoes in my heart! It is a song of Fanchonette:

In vain, in vain; we meet no more,

Nor dream what fates befall;

And long upon the stranger's shore

My voice on thee may call,

When years have clothed the line in moss

That tells thy name and days,

And withered, on thy simple cross,

The wreaths of Pere la Chaise!

XVI

THE MALADY CALLED CATALOGITIS

Judge Methuen tells me that one of the most pleasing delusions he has experienced in his long and active career as a bibliomaniac is that which is born of the catalogue habit. Presuming that there are among my readers many laymen,—for I preach salvation to the heathen,—I will explain for their information that the catalogue habit, so called, is a practice to which the confirmed lover of books is likely to become addicted. It is a custom of many publishers and dealers to publish and to disseminate at certain periods lists of their wares, in the hope of thereby enticing readers to buy those wares.

By what means these crafty tradesmen secure the names of their prospective victims I cannot say, but this I know full well—that there seems not to be a book-lover on the face of the earth, I care not how remote or how secret his habitation may be, that these dealers do not presently find him out and overwhelm him with their delightful temptations.

I have been told that among booksellers there exists a secret league which provides for the interchange of confidences; so that when a new customer enters a shop in the Fulham road or in Oxford street or along the quays of Paris, or it matters not where (so long as the object of his inquiry be a book), within the space of a month that man's name and place of residence are reported to and entered in the address list of every other bookseller in Christendom, and forthwith and forever after the catalogues and price-lists and bulletins of publishers and dealers in every part of the world are pelted at him through the unerring processes of the mails.

Judge Methuen has been a victim (a pleasant victim) to the catalogue habit for the last forty years, and he has declared that if all the catalogues sent to and read by him in that space of time were gathered together in a heap they would make a pile bigger than Pike's Peak, and a thousandfold more interesting. I myself have been a famous reader of catalogues, and I can testify that the habit has possessed me of remarkable delusions, the most conspicuous of which is that which produces within me the conviction that a book is as good as mine as soon as I have met with its title in a catalogue, and set an X over against it in pencil.

I recall that on one occasion I was discussing with Judge Methuen and Dr. O'Rell the attempted escapes of Charles I. from Carisbrooke Castle; a point of difference having arisen, I said: "Gentlemen, I will refer to Hillier's 'Narrative,' and I doubt not that my argument will be sustained by that authority."

It was vastly easier, however, to cite Hillier than it was to find him. For three days I searched in my library, and tumbled my books about in that confusion which results from undue eagerness; 't was all in vain; neither hide nor hair of the desired volume could I discover. It finally occurred to me that I must have lent the book to somebody, and then again I felt sure that it had been stolen.

No tidings of the missing volume came to me, and I had almost forgotten the incident when one evening (it was fully two years after my discussion with my cronies) I came upon, in one of the drawers of my oak chest, a Sotheran catalogue of May, 1871. By the merest chance I opened it, and as luck would have it, I opened it at the very page upon which appeared this item:

"Hillier (G.) 'Narrative of the Attempted Escapes of Charles the First from Carisbrooke Castle'; cr. 8vo, 1852, cloth, 3/6."

Against this item appeared a cross in my chirography, and I saw at a glance that this was my long-lost Hillier! I had meant to buy it, and had marked it for purchase; but with the determination and that pencilled cross the transaction had ended. Yet, having resolved to buy it had served me almost as effectively as though I had actually bought it; I thought—aye, I could have sworn—I HAD bought it, simply because I MEANT to buy it.

"The experience is not unique," said Judge Methuen, when I narrated it to him at our next meeting. "Speaking for myself, I can say that it is a confirmed habit with me to mark certain items in catalogues which I read, and then to go my way in the pleasing conviction that they are actually mine."

"I meet with cases of this character continually," said Dr. O'Rell. "The hallucination is one that is recognized as a specific one by pathologists; its cure is quickest effected by means of hypnotism. Within the last year a lady of beauty and refinement came to me in serious distress. She confided to me amid a copious effusion of tears that her husband was upon the verge of insanity. Her testimony was to the effect that the unfortunate man believed himself to be possessed of a large library, the fact being that the number of his books was limited to three hundred or thereabouts.

"Upon inquiry I learned that N. M. (for so I will call the victim of this delusion) made a practice of reading and of marking booksellers' catalogues; further investigation developed that N. M.'s great-uncle on his mother's side had invented a flying-machine that would not fly, and that a half-brother of his was the author of a pamphlet entitled '16 to 1; or the Poor Man's Vade-Mecum.'

"'Madam,' said I, 'it is clear to me that your husband is afflicted with catalogitis.'

"At this the poor woman went into hysterics, bewailing that she should have lived to see the object of her affection the victim of a malady so grievous as to require a Greek name. When she became calmer I explained to her that the malady was by no means fatal, and that it yielded readily to treatment."

"What, in plain terms," asked Judge Methuen, "is catalogitis?"

"I will explain briefly," answered the doctor. "You must know first that every perfect human being is provided with two sets of bowels; he has physical bowels and intellectual bowels, the brain being the latter. Hippocrates (since whose time the science of medicine has not advanced even the two stadia, five parasangs of Xenophon)—Hippocrates, I say, discovered that the brain is subject to those very same diseases to which the other and inferior bowels are liable.

"Galen confirmed this discovery and he records a case (Lib. xi., p. 318) wherein there were exhibited in the intellectual bowels symptoms similar to those we find in appendicitis. The brain is wrought into certain convolutions, just as the alimentary canal is; the fourth layer, so called, contains elongated groups of small cells or nuclei, radiating at right angles to its plane, which groups present a distinctly fanlike structure. Catalogitis is a stoppage of this fourth layer, whereby the functions of the fanlike structure are suffered no longer to cool the brain, and whereby also continuity of thought is interrupted, just as continuity of digestion is prevented by stoppage of the vermiform appendix.

"The learned Professor Biersteintrinken," continued Dr. O'Rell, "has advanced in his scholarly work on 'Raderinderkopf' the interesting theory that catalogitis is produced by the presence in the brain of a germ which has its origin in the cheap paper used by booksellers for catalogue purposes, and this theory seems to have the approval of M. Marie-Tonsard, the most famous of authorities on inebriety, in his celebrated classic entitled 'Un Trait sur Jacques-Jacques.'"

"Did you effect a cure in the case of N. M.?" I asked.

"With the greatest of ease," answered the doctor. "By means of hypnotism I purged his intellectuals of their hallucination, relieving them of their perception of objects which have no reality and ridding them of sensations which have no corresponding external cause. The patient made a rapid recovery, and, although three months have elapsed since his discharge, he has had no return of the disease."

As a class booksellers do not encourage the reading of other booksellers' catalogues; this is, presumably, because they do not care to encourage buyers to buy of other sellers. My bookseller, who in all virtues of head and heart excels all other booksellers I ever met with, makes a scrupulous practice of destroying the catalogues that come to his shop, lest some stray copy may fall into the hands of a mousing book-lover and divert his attention to other hunting-grounds. It is indeed remarkable to what excess the catalogue habit will carry its victim; the author of "Will Shakespeare, a Comedy," has frequently confessed to me that it mattered not to him whether a catalogue was twenty years old—so long as it was a catalogue of books he found the keenest delight in its perusal; I have often heard Mr. Hamlin, the theatre manager, say that he preferred old catalogues to new, for the reason that the bargains to be met with in old catalogues expired long ago under the statute of limitations.

Judge Methuen, who is a married man and has therefore had an excellent opportunity to study the sex, tells me that the wives of bibliomaniacs regard catalogues as the most mischievous temptations that can be thrown in the way of their husbands. I once committed the imprudence of mentioning the subject in Mrs. Methuen's presence: that estimable lady gave it as her opinion that there were plenty of ways of spending money foolishly without having recourse to a book-catalogue for suggestion. I wonder whether Captivity would have had this opinion, had Providence ordained that we should walk together the quiet pathway of New England life; would Yseult always have retained the exuberance and sweetness of her youth, had she and I realized what might have been? Would Fanchonette always have sympathized with the whims and vagaries of the restless yet loyal soul that hung enraptured on her singing in the Quartier Latin so long ago that the memory of that song is like the memory of a ghostly echo now?

Away with such reflections! Bring in the candles, good servitor, and range them at my bed's head; sweet avocation awaits me, for here I have a goodly parcel of catalogues with which to commune. They are messages from Methuen, Sotheran, Libbie, Irvine, Hutt, Davey, Baer, Crawford, Bangs, McClurg, Matthews, Francis, Bouton, Scribner, Benjamin, and a score of other friends in every part of Christendom; they deserve and they shall have my respectful—nay, my enthusiastic attention. Once more I shall seem to be in the old familiar shops where treasures abound and where patient delving bringeth rich rewards. Egad, what a spendthrift I shall be this night; pence, shillings, thalers, marks, francs, dollars, sovereigns—they are the same to me!

Then, after I have comprehended all the treasures within reach, how sweet shall be my dreams of shelves overflowing with the wealth of which my fancy has possessed me!

Then shall my library be devote

To the magic of Niddy-Noddy,

Including the volumes which Nobody wrote

And the works of Everybody.

XVII

THE NAPOLEONIC RENAISSANCE

If I had begun collecting Napoleonana in my youth I should now have on hand a priceless collection. This reminds me that when I first came to Chicago suburban property along the North Shore could be bought for five hundred dollars an acre which now sells for two hundred dollars a front foot; if I had purchased real estate in that locality when I had the opportunity forty years ago I should be a millionnaire at the present time.

I think I am more regretful of having neglected the Napoleonana than of having missed the real-estate chances, for since my library contains fewer than two hundred volumes relating to Bonaparte and his times I feel that I have been strangely remiss in the pursuit of one of the most interesting and most instructive of bibliomaniac fads. When I behold the remarkable collections of Napoleonana made by certain friends of mine I am filled with conflicting emotions of delight and envy, and Judge Methuen and I are wont to contemplate with regret the opportunities we once had of throwing all these modern collections in the shade.

When I speak of Napoleonana I refer exclusively to literature relating to Napoleon; the term, however, is generally used in a broader sense, and includes every variety of object, from the snuff-boxes used by the emperor at Malmaison to the slippers he wore at St. Helena. My friend, Mr. Redding, of California, has a silver knife and fork that once belonged to Bonaparte, and Mr. Mills, another friend of mine, has the neckerchief which

Napoleon wore on the field of Waterloo. In Le Blanc's little treatise upon the art of tying the cravat it is recorded that Napoleon generally wore a black silk cravat, as was remarked at Wagram, Lodi, Marengo and Austerlitz. "But at Waterloo," says Le Blanc, "it was observed that, contrary to his usual custom, he wore a white handkerchief with a flowing bow, although the day previous he appeared in his black cravat."

I remember to have seen in the collection of Mr. Melville E. Stone a finger-ring, which, having been brought by an old French soldier to New Orleans, ultimately found its way to a pawn-shop. This bauble was of gold, and at two opposite points upon its outer surface appeared a Napoleonic "N," done in black enamel: by pressing upon one of these Ns a secret spring was operated, the top of the ring flew back, and a tiny gold figure of the Little Corporal stood up, to the astonishment and admiration of the beholder.

Another curious Napoleonic souvenir in Mr. Stone's motley collection is a cotton print handkerchief, upon which are recorded scenes from the career of the emperor; the thing must have been of English manufacture, for only an Englishman (inspired by that fear and that hatred of Bonaparte which only Englishmen had) could have devised this atrocious libel. One has to read the literature current in the earlier part of this century in order to get a correct idea of the terror with which Bonaparte filled his enemies, and this literature is so extensive that it seems an impossibility that anything like a complete collection should be got together; to say nothing of the histories, the biographies, the volumes of reminiscence and the books of criticism which the career of the Corsican inspired, there are Napoleon dream-books, Napoleon song-books, Napoleon chap-books, etc., etc., beyond the capability of enumeration.

The English were particularly active in disseminating libels upon Napoleon; they charged him in their books and pamphlets with murder, arson, incest, treason, treachery, cowardice, seduction, hypocrisy, avarice, robbery, ingratitude, and jealousy; they said that he poisoned his sick soldiers, that he was the father of Hortense's child, that he committed the most atrocious cruelties in Egypt and Italy, that he married Barras' discarded mistress, that he was afflicted with a loathsome disease, that he murdered the Duc d'Enghien and officers in his own army of whom he was jealous, that he was criminally intimate with his own sisters—in short, there was no crime, however revolting, with which these calumniators were not hasty to charge the emperor.

This same vindictive hatred was visited also upon all associated with Bonaparte in the conduct of affairs at that time. Murat was "a brute and a thief"; Josephine, Hortense, Pauline, and Mme. Letitia were courtesans; Berthier was a shuffling, time-serving lackey and tool; Augereau was a bastard, a spy, a robber, and a murderer; Fouche was the incarnation of every vice; Lucien Bonaparte was a roue and a marplot; Cambaceres was a debauchee; Lannes was a thief, brigand, and a poisoner; Talleyrand and Barras were—well, what evil was told of them has yet to be disproved. But you would gather from contemporaneous English publications that Bonaparte and his associates were veritable fiends from hell sent to scourge civilization. These books are so strangely curious that we find it hard to classify them: we cannot call them history, and they are too truculent to pass for humor; yet they occupy a distinct and important place among Napoleonana.

Until William Hazlitt's life of Bonaparte appeared we had no English treatment of Bonaparte that was in any sense fair, and, by the way, Hazlitt's work is the only one in English I know of which gives the will of Bonaparte, an exceedingly interesting document.

For a good many years I held the character of Napoleon in light esteem, for the reason that he had but small regard for books. Recent revelations, however, made to me by Dr. O'Rell (grandnephew of "Tom Burke of Ours"), have served to dissipate that prejudice, and I question not that I shall duly become as ardent a worshipper of the Corsican as my doctor himself is. Dr. O'Rell tells me—and his declarations are corroborated by Frederic Masson and other authorities—that Bonaparte was a lover and a collector of books, and that he contributed largely to the dignity and the glorification of literature by publishing a large number of volumes in the highest style of the art.

The one department of literature for which he seems to have had no liking was fiction. Novels of all kinds he was in the habit of tossing into the fire. He was a prodigious buyer of books, and those which he read were invariably stamped on the outer cover with the imperial arms; at St. Helena his library stamp was merely a seal upon which ink was smeared.

Napoleon cared little for fine bindings, yet he knew their value, and whenever a presentation copy was to be bound he required that it be bound handsomely. The books in his own library were invariably bound "in calf of indifferent quality," and he was wont, while reading a book, to fill the margin with comments in pencil. Wherever he went he took a library of books with him, and these volumes he had deprived of all superfluous margin, so as to save weight and space. Not infrequently when hampered by the rapid growth of this travelling library he would toss the "overflow" of books out of his carriage window, and it was his custom (I shudder to record it!) to separate the leaves of pamphlets, magazines, and volumes by running his finger between them, thereby invariably tearing the pages in shocking wise.

In the arrangement of his library Napoleon observed that exacting method which was characteristic of him in other employments and avocations. Each book had its particular place in a special case, and Napoleon knew his library so well that he could at any moment place his hand upon any volume he desired. The libraries at his palaces he had arranged exactly as the library at Malmaison was, and never was one book borrowed from one to serve in another. It is narrated of him that if ever a volume was missing Napoleon would describe its size and the color of its binding to the librarian, and would point out the place where it might have been wrongly put and the case where it properly belonged.

If any one question the greatness of this man let him explain if he can why civilization's interest in Napoleon increases as time rolls on. Why is it that we are curious to know all about him—that we have gratification in hearing tell of his minutest habits, his moods, his whims, his practices, his prejudices? Why is it that even those who hated him and who denied his genius have felt called upon to record in ponderous tomes their reminiscences of him and his deeds? Princes, generals, lords, courtiers, poets, painters, priests, plebeians—all have vied with one another in answering humanity's demand for more and more and ever more about Napoleon Bonaparte.

I think that the supply will, like the demand, never be exhausted. The women of the court have supplied us with their memoirs; so have the diplomats of that period; so have the wives of his generals; so have the Tom-Dick-and-Harry spectators of those kaleidoscopic scenes; so have his keepers in exile; so has his barber. The chambermaids will be heard from in good time, and the hostlers, and the scullions. Already there are rumors that we are soon to be regaled with Memoirs of the Emperor Napoleon by the Lady who knew the Tailor who Once Sewed a Button on the Emperor's Coat, edited by her loving grandson, the Duc de Bunco.

Without doubt many of those who read these lines will live to see the time when memoirs of Napoleon will be offered by "a gentleman who purchased a collection of Napoleon spoons in 1899"; doubtless, too, the book will be hailed with satisfaction, for this Napoleonic enthusiasm increases as time wears on.

Curious, is it not, that no calm, judicial study of this man's character and exploits is received with favor? He who treats of the subject must be either a hater or an adorer of Napoleon; his blood must be hot with the enthusiasm of rage or of love.

To the human eye there appears in space a luminous sphere that in its appointed path goes on unceasingly. The wise men are not agreed whether this apparition is merely of gaseous composition or is a solid body supplied extraneously with heat and luminosity, inexhaustibly; some argue that its existence will be limited to the period of one thousand, or five hundred thousand, or one million years; others declare that it will roll on until the end of time. Perhaps the nature of that luminous sphere will never be truly known to mankind; yet with calm dignity it moves in its appointed path among the planets and the stars of the universe, its fires unabated, its luminosity undimmed.

Even so the great Corsican, scrutinized of all human eyes, passes along the aisle of Time enveloped in the impenetrable mystery of enthusiasm, genius, and splendor.

XVIII

MY WORKSHOP AND OTHERS

The women-folk are few up there,

For 't were not fair, you know,

That they our heavenly bliss should share

Who vex us here below!

The few are those who have been kind

To husbands such as we:

They knew our fads and didn't mind—

Says Dibdin's ghost to me.

It has never been explained to my satisfaction why women, as a class, are the enemies of books, and are particularly hostile to bibliomania. The exceptions met with now and then simply prove the rule. Judge Methuen declares that bibliophobia is but one phase of jealousy; that one's wife hates one's books because she fears that her husband is in love, or is going to be in love, with those companions of his student hours. If, instead of being folios, quartos, octavos, and the like, the Judge's books were buxom, blithe maidens, his wife could hardly be more jealous of the Judge's attentions to them than she is under existing circumstances. On one occasion, having found the Judge on two successive afternoons sitting alone in the library with Pliny in his lap, this spirited lady snatched the insidious volume from her husband's embraces and locked it up in one of the kitchen pantries; nor did she release the object of her displeasure until the Judge had promised solemnly to be more circumspect in the future, and had further mollified his wife's anger by bringing home a new silk dress and a bonnet of exceptional loveliness.

Other instances of a similar character have demonstrated that Mrs. Methuen regards with implacable antipathy the volumes upon which my learned and ingenious friend would fain lavish the superabundance of his affection. Many years ago the Judge was compelled to resort to every kind of artifice in order to sneak new books into his house, and had he not been imbued with the true afflatus of bibliomania he would long ago have broken down under the heartless tyranny of his vindictive spouse.

When I look around me and survey the persecution to which book-lovers are subjected by their wives, I thank the goddess Fortune that she has cast my lot among the celibates; indeed, it is still one of the few serious questions

I have not yet solved, viz.: whether a man can at the same time be true to a wife and to bibliomania. Both are exacting mistresses, and neither will tolerate a rival.

Dr. O'Rell has a theory that the trouble with most wives is that they are not caught young enough; he quotes Dr. Johnson's sage remark to the effect that "much can be made of a Scotchman if caught young," and he asserts that this is equally true of woman. Mrs. O'Rell was a mere girl when she wedded with the doctor, and the result of thirty years' experience and training is that this model woman sympathizes with her excellent husband's tastes, and actually has a feeling of contempt for other wives who have never heard of Father Prout and Kit North, and who object to their husbands' smoking in bed.

I recall with what enthusiasm I once heard this superior creature commend the doctor for having accepted in lieu of a fee a set of Calvin's "Institutes," with copious notes, in twelve octavo volumes, and a portfolio of colored fox-hunting prints. My admiration for this model wife could find expression in no other way; I jumped from my chair, seized her in my arms, and imprinted upon her brow a fervent but respectful kiss.

It would be hard to imagine a prettier picture than that presented to my vision as I looked in from the porch of the doctor's residence upon the doctor's family gathered together in the library after dinner. The doctor himself, snuggled down in a vast easy-chair, was dividing his attention between a brier pipe and the odes of Propertius; his wife, beside him in her rocker, smiled and smiled again over the quaint humor of Mrs. Gaskell's "Cranford"; upon yonder settee, Francis Mahony Methuen, the oldest son, was deep in the perusal of Wilson's "Tales of the Border";

his brother, Russell Lowell, was equally absorbed in the pathetic tale of "The Man without a Country"; Letitia Landon Methuen, the daughter, was quietly sobbing over the tragedy of "Evangeline"; in his high chair sat the chubby baby boy, Beranger Methuen, crowing gleefully over an illustrated copy of that grand old classic, "Poems for Infant Minds by Two Young Persons."

For several moments I stood spellbound, regarding with ineffable rapture this inspiring spectacle. "How manifold are thy blessings, O Bibliomania," thought I, "and how graciously they are distributed in this joyous circle, wherein it is permitted to see not only the maturer members, but, alas, the youth and even the babes and sucklings drinking freely and gratefully at the fountain-head of thy delights!"

Dr. O'Rell's library is one of the most charming apartments I know of. It looks out upon every variety of scenery, for Dr. O'Rell has had constructed at considerable expense a light iron framework from which are suspended at different times cunningly painted canvases representing landscapes and marines corresponding to the most whimsical fancy.

In the dead of winter, the doctor often has a desire to look out upon a cheery landscape; thereupon, by a simple manipulation of a keyboard, there is unrolled a panorama of velvety hillsides and flowery meads, of grazing sheep, and of piping rustics; so natural is the spectacle that one can almost hear the music of the reeds, and fancy himself in Arcadia. If in midsummer the heat is oppressive and life seems burthensome, forthwith another canvas is outspread, and the glories of the Alps appear, or a stretch of blue sea, or a corner of a primeval forest.

So there is an outlook for every mood, and I doubt not that this ingenious provision contributes potently towards promoting bibliomaniac harmony and prosperity in my friend's household. It is true that I myself am not susceptible to external influences when once I am surrounded by books; I do not care a fig whether my library overlooks a garden or a desert; give me my dear companions in their dress of leather, cloth, or boards, and it matters not to me whether God sends storm or sunshine, flowers or hail, light or darkness, noise or calm. Yet I know and admit that environment means much to most people, and I do most heartily applaud Dr. O'Rell's versatile device.

I have always thought that De Quincey's workshop would have given me great delight. The particular thing that excited De Quincey's choler was interference with his books and manuscripts, which he piled atop of one another upon the floor and over his desk, until at last there would be but a narrow little pathway from the desk to the fireplace and from the fireplace to the door; and his writing-table— gracious! what a Pelion upon Ossa of confusion it must have been!

Yet De Quincey insisted that he knew "just where everything was," and he merely exacted that the servants attempt no such vandalism as "cleaning up" in his workshop. Of course there would presently come a time when there was no more room on the table and when the little pathway to the fireplace and the door would be no longer visible; then, with a sigh, De Quincey would lock the door of that room and betake himself to other quarters, which in turn would eventually become quite as littered up, cluttered up, and impassable as the first rooms.

From all that can be gathered upon the subject it would appear that De Quincey was careless in his treatment of books; I have read somewhere (but I forget where) that he used his forefinger as a paper-cutter and that he did not hesitate to mutilate old folios which he borrowed. But he was extraordinarily tender with his manuscripts; and he was wont to carry in his pockets a soft brush with which he used to dust off his manuscripts most carefully before handing them to the publisher.

Sir Walter Scott was similarly careful with his books, and he used, for purposes of dusting them, the end of a fox's tail set in a handle of silver. Scott, was, however, particular and systematic in the arrangement of his books, and his workroom, with its choice bric-a-brac and its interesting collection of pictures and framed letters, was a veritable paradise to the visiting book-lover and curio-lover. He was as fond of early rising as Francis Jeffrey was averse to it, and both these eminent men were strongly attached to animal pets. Jeffrey particularly affected an aged and garrulous parrot and an equally disreputable little dog. Scott was so stanch a friend of dogs that wherever he went he was accompanied by one or two—sometimes by a whole kennel—of these faithful brutes.

In Mrs. Gordon's noble "Memoirs" we have a vivid picture of Professor Wilson's workroom. All was confusion there: "his room was a strange mixture of what may be called order and untidiness, for there was not a scrap of paper or a book that his hand could not light upon in a moment, while to the casual eye, in search of discovery, it would appear chaos." Wilson had no love for fine furniture, and he seems to have crowded his books together without regard to any system of classification. He had a habit of mixing his books around with fishing-tackle, and his charming biographer tells us it was no uncommon thing to find the "Wealth of Nations," "Boxiana," the "Faerie Queen," Jeremy Taylor, and Ben Jonson occupying close quarters with fishing-rods, boxing-gloves, and tins of barley-sugar.

Charles Lamb's favorite workshop was in an attic; upon the walls of this room he and his sister pasted old prints and gay pictures, and this resulted in giving the place a cheery aspect. Lamb loved old books, old friends, old times; "he evades the present, he works at the future, and his affections revert to and settle on the past,"—so says Hazlitt. His favorite books seem to have been Bunyan's "Holy War," Browne's "Urn-Burial," Burton's "Anatomy of Melancholy," Fuller's "Worthies," and Taylor's "Holy Living and Dying." Thomas Westwood tells us that there were few modern volumes in his library, it being his custom to give away and throw away (as the same writer asserts) presentation copies of contemporaneous literature. Says Barry Cornwall: "Lamb's pleasures lay amongst the books of the old English writers," and Lamb himself uttered these memorable words: "I cannot sit and think—books think for me."

Wordsworth, on the other hand, cared little for books; his library was a small one, embracing hardly more than five hundred volumes. He drew his inspiration not from books, but from Nature. From all that I have heard of him I judge him to have been a very dull man. Allibone relates of him that he once remarked that he did not consider himself a witty poet. "Indeed," quoth he, "I don't think I ever was witty but once in my life."

His friends urged him to tell them about it. After some hesitation, he said: "Well, I will tell you. I was standing some time ago at the entrance of Rydal Mount. A man accosted me with the question: 'Pray, sir, have you seen my wife pass by?' Whereupon I retorted, 'Why, my good friend, I didn't know till this moment that you had a wife.'"

Illustrative of Wordsworth's vanity, it is told that when it was reported that the next Waverley novel was to be "Rob Roy," the poet took down his "Ballads" and read to the company "Rob Roy's Grave." Then he said gravely: "I do not know what more Mr. Scott can have to say on the subject."

Wordsworth and Dickens disliked each other cordially. Having been asked his opinion of the young novelist, Wordsworth answered: "Why, I'm not much given to turn critic on people I meet; but, as you ask me, I will cordially avow that I thought him a very talkative young person—but I dare say he may be very clever. Mind, I don't want to say a word against him, for I have never read a line he has written."

The same inquirer subsequently asked Dickens how he liked Wordsworth.

"Like him!" roared Dickens, "not at all; he is a dreadful Old Ass!"

XIX

OUR DEBT TO MONKISH MEN

Where one has the time and the money to devote to the collection of missals and illuminated books, the avocation must be a very delightful one. I never look upon a missal or upon a bit of antique illumination that I do not invest that object with a certain poetic romance, and I picture to myself long lines of monkish men bending over their tasks, and applying themselves with pious enthusiasm thereto. We should not flatter ourselves that the enjoyment of the delights of bibliomania was reserved to one time and generation; a greater than any of us lived many centuries ago, and went his bibliomaniacal way, gathering together treasures from every quarter, and diffusing every where a veneration and love for books.

Richard de Bury was the king, if not the father, of bibliomaniacs; his immortal work reveals to us that long before the invention of printing men were tormented and enraptured by those very same desires, envies, jealousies, greeds, enthusiasms, and passions which possess and control bibliomaniacs at the present time. That vanity was sometimes the controlling passion with the early collectors is evidenced in a passage in Barclay's satire, "The Ship of Fools"; there are the stanzas which apply so neatly to certain people I know that sometimes I actually suspect that Barclay's prophetic eye must have had these nineteenth-century charlatans in view.

But yet I have them in great reverence

And honor, saving them from filth and ordure

By often brushing and much diligence.

Full goodly bound in pleasant coverture

Of damask, satin, or else of velvet pure,

I keep them sure, fearing lest they should be lost,

For in them is the cunning wherein I me boast.

But if it fortune that any learned man

Within my house fall to disputation,

I draw the curtains to show my books them,

That they of my cunning should make probation;

I love not to fall into altercation,

And while they come, my books I turn and wind,

For all is in them, and nothing in my mind.

Richard de Bury had exceptional opportunities for gratifying his bibliomaniac passions. He was chancellor and treasurer of Edward III., and his official position gained him access to public and private libraries and to the society of literary men. Moreover, when it became known that he was fond of such things, people from every quarter sent him and brought him old books; it may be that they hoped in this wise to court his official favor, or perhaps they were prompted by the less selfish motive of gladdening the bibliomaniac soul.

"The flying fame of our love," says de Bury, "had already spread in all directions, and it was reported not only that we had a longing desire for books, and especially for old ones, but that any one could more easily obtain our favors by quartos than by money. Wherefore, when supported by the bounty of the aforesaid prince of worthy memory, we were enabled to oppose or advance, to appoint or to discharge; crazy quartos and tottering folios, precious however in our sight as in our affections, flowed in most rapidly from the great and the small, instead of new year's gifts and remunerations, and instead of presents and jewels. Then the cabinets of the most noble monasteries were opened, cases were unlocked, caskets were unclasped, and sleeping volumes which had slumbered for long ages in their sepulchres were roused up, and those that lay hid in dark places were overwhelmed with the rays of a new light. Among these, as time served, we sat down more voluptuously than the delicate physician could do amidst his stores of aromatics, and where we found an object of love we found also an assuagement."

"If," says de Bury, "we would have amassed cups of gold and silver, excellent horses, or no mean sums of money, we could in those days have laid up abundance of wealth for ourselves. But we regarded books, not pounds; and valued codices more than florins, and preferred paltry pamphlets to pampered palfreys. On tedious embassies and in perilous times, we carried about with us that fondness for books which many waters could not extinguish."

And what books they were in those old days! What tall folios! What stout quartos! How magnificent were the bindings, wrought often in silver devices, sometimes in gold, and not infrequently in silver and gold, with splendid jewels and precious stones to add their value to that of the precious volume which they adorned. The works of Justin, Seneca, Martial, Terence, and Claudian were highly popular with the bibliophiles of early times; and the writings of Ovid, Tully, Horace, Cato, Aristotle, Sallust, Hippocrates, Macrobius, Augustine, Bede, Gregory, Origen, etc. But for the veneration and love for books which the monks of the mediaeval ages had, what would have been preserved to us of the classics of the Greeks and the Romans?

The same auspicious fate that prompted those bibliomaniacal monks to hide away manuscript treasures in the cellars of their monasteries, inspired Poggio Bracciolini several centuries later to hunt out and invade those sacred hiding-places, and these quests were rewarded with finds whose value cannot be overestimated. All that we have of the histories of Livy come to us through Poggio's industry as a manuscript-hunter; this same worthy found and brought away from different monasteries a perfect copy of Quintilian, a Cicero's oration for Caecina, a complete Tertullian, a Petronius Arbiter, and fifteen or twenty other classics almost as valuable as those I have named. From German monasteries, Poggio's friend, Nicolas of Treves, brought away twelve comedies of Plautus and a fragment of Aulus Gellius.

Dear as their pagan books were to the monkish collectors, it was upon their Bibles, their psalters, and their other religious books that these mediaeval bibliomaniacs expended their choicest art and their most loving care. St. Cuthbert's "Gospels," preserved in the British Museum, was written by Egfrith, a monk, circa 720; Aethelwald bound the book in gold and precious stones, and Bilfrid, a hermit, illuminated it by prefixing to each gospel a beautiful painting representing one of the Evangelists, and a tessellated cross, executed in a most elaborate manner. Bilfrid also illuminated the large capital letters at the beginning of the gospels. This precious volume was still further enriched by Aldred of Durham, who interlined it with a Saxon Gloss, or version of the Latin text of St. Jerome.

"Of the exact pecuniary value of books during the middle ages," says Merryweather, "we have no means of judging. The few instances that have accidentally been recorded are totally inadequate to enable us to form an opinion. The extravagant estimate given by some as to the value of books in those days is merely conjectural, as it necessarily must be when we remember that the price was guided by the accuracy of the transcription, the splendor of the binding (which was often gorgeous to excess), and by the beauty and richness of the illuminations. Many of the manuscripts of the middle ages are magnificent in the extreme; sometimes inscribed in liquid gold on parchment of the richest purple, and adorned with illuminations of exquisite workmanship."

With such a veneration and love for books obtaining in the cloister and at the fireside, what pathos is revealed to us in the supplication which invited God's blessing upon the beloved tomes: "O Lord, send the virtue of thy Holy Spirit upon these our books; that cleansing them from all earthly things, by thy holy blessing, they may mercifully enlighten our hearts and give us true understanding; and grant that by thy teachings they may brightly preserve and make full an abundance of good works according to thy will."

And what inspiration and cheer does every book-lover find in the letter which that grand old bibliomaniac, Alcuin, addressed to Charlemagne: "I, your Flaccus, according to your admonitions and good will, administer to some in the house of St. Martin the sweets of the Holy Scriptures; others I inebriate with the study of ancient wisdom; and others I fill with the fruits of grammatical lore. Many I seek to instruct in the order of the stars which illuminate the glorious vault of heaven, so that they may be made ornaments to the holy church of God and the court of your imperial majesty; that the goodness of God and your kindness may not be altogether unproductive of good. But in doing this I discover the want of much, especially those exquisite books of scholastic learning which I possessed in my own country, through the industry of my good and most devout master, Egbert. I therefore entreat your Excellence to permit me to send into Britain some of our youths to procure those books which we so much desire, and thus transplant into France the flowers of Britain, that they may fructify and perfume, not only the garden at York, but also the Paradise of Tours, and that we may say in the words of the song: 'Let my beloved come into his garden and eat his pleasant fruit;' and to the young: 'Eat, O friends; drink, yea, drink abundantly, O beloved;' or exhort in the words of the prophet Isaiah: 'Every one that thirsteth to come to the waters, and ye that have no money, come ye, buy and eat: yea, come buy wine and milk, without money and without price.'"

I was meaning to have somewhat to say about Alcuin, and had intended to pay my respects to Canute, Alfred, the Abbot of St. Albans, the Archbishop of Salzburg, the Prior of Dover, and other mediaeval worthies, when Judge Methuen came in and interrupted the thread of my meditation. The Judge brings me some verses done recently by a poet-friend of his, and he asks me to give them a place in these memoirs as illustrating the vanity of human confidence.

One day I got a missive

Writ in a dainty hand,

Which made my manly bosom

With vanity expand.

'T was from a "young admirer"

Who asked me would I mind

Sending her "favorite poem"

"In autograph, and signed."

She craved the boon so sweetly

That I had been a churl

Had I repulsed the homage

Of this gentle, timid girl;

With bright illuminations

I decked the manuscript,

And in my choicest paints and inks

My brush and pen I dipt.

Indeed it had been tedious

But that a flattered smile

Played on my rugged features

And eased my toil the while.

I was assured my poem

Would fill her with delight—

I fancied she was pretty—

I knew that she was bright!

And for a spell thereafter

That unknown damsel's face

With its worshipful expression

Pursued me every place;

Meseemed to hear her whisper:

"O, thank you, gifted sir,

For the overwhelming honor

You so graciously confer!"

But a catalogue from Benjamin's

Disproves what things meseemed—

Dispels with savage certainty

The flattering dreams I dreamed;

For that poor "favorite poem,"

Done and signed in autograph,

Is listed in "Cheap Items"

At a dollar-and-a-half.

Made in the USA
Columbia, SC
09 January 2025